108865

048260

10855670

COLOSSEUM

COLOSSEUM

ROME'S ARENA OF DEATH

Peter Connolly

Published to accompany the television programme
Colosseum, first broadcast on BBC1 in 2003.
Producer and director: Tilman Remme
Executive producers: Jonathan Stamp
and Laurence Rees

First published 2003
Copyright © Peter Connolly
The moral right of the author has been asserted.

All rights reserved. No part of this book may be
reproduced in any form or by any means without prior
written permission from the publisher, except by a
reviewer who may quote brief passages in a review.

ISBN 0 563 48892 1

Published by BBC Books, BBC Worldwide Ltd,
Woodlands, 80 Wood Lane, London W12 0TT

Commissioning editor: Sally Potter
Project editor: Christopher Tinker
Copy-editor: Judith Scott
Art director: Linda Blakemore
Designer: Bill Mason
Picture researcher: Sarah Hopper

Set in Foundry Old Style
Printed and bound in Great Britain by
Butler & Tanner Ltd, Frome
Colour separations by Radstock Reproductions Ltd,
Midsomer Norton
Jacket printed by Lawrence-Allen Ltd,
Weston-super-Mare

ACKNOWLEDGEMENTS

I would like to thank the following for their
help in writing this book: Peter Hill for his
advice on the building techniques and materials;
Amanda Claridge for looking over the chapters
on the archaeology and the later history of the
Colosseum; John Elms for his advice on the water
supply for the *naumachia*; Heinz-Jurgen Beste for
his help and encouragement when I was working
in the basement of the Colosseum; the director
and staff of the British School at Rome, in
particular Maria Pia Malvezzi, who arranged for
me to study in the Colosseum and to examine
the gladiator armour at Naples; the staff at the
Library of Greek and Roman Studies in London,
in particular Sue Willetts and Paul Jackson, for
their help in finding obscure articles and books;
and finally the Soprintendenza Archeologica
at Rome.

Peter Connolly, October 2003

Page 1: A bronze statuette of a *retiarius* with his trident
from Esbarres in France.

CONTENTS

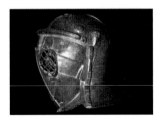

INTRODUCTION

I was working in the basement below the arena of the Colosseum one Easter when I heard the strains of 'Ave, Ave, Ave Maria' wafting down to me. A small group of pilgrims had gathered to remember the Christian martyrs who had suffered and died there for their beliefs, nearly two thousand years ago.

The Colosseum is the most impressive, and the most notorious, of Rome's classical ruins, a building forever associated with death and gory spectacle. Some years ago, when I decided to investigate how the world's most famous amphitheatre had functioned, a colleague said to me, 'Why glorify that disgusting place?' It often provokes that sort of reaction, but to the millions of visitors who have been drawn there over the years it still holds a gruesome fascination.

Many of us look upon the ancient Romans with ambivalence. We may admire their achievements as a sophisticated civilization while abhorring the brutality of a society that built a huge and powerful empire based on warmongering, slavery, tyranny and torture. When we think about the Colosseum and the gladiatorial games that took place there most of us think of the popular Hollywood image of the mob, urged on by a mad emperor, baying for blood. But is modern society so very different? We all have an instinct for violence, even if most of us manage to control it most of the time. Bear-baiting, bull-fighting, foxhunting, hare-coursing – blood sports have been popular since the beginning of time. Some countries still allow public executions, and we have only to look back 135 years or so to Thomas Hardy (who died in 1928) to find an Englishman who witnessed a public hanging.

And just as public executions were always bound to draw not just the common rabble but people from all corners of society, so did the blood-thirsty gladiatorial games in ancient Rome. They were not put on just to please the lower classes, as is sometimes claimed. There are plenty of examples of mosaics and bas-reliefs that came from wealthy people's houses or tombs glorifying the gladiators, and their images have been found on everyday household items, such as vases, lamps and bone knife-handles. One would perhaps expect that most Roman intellectuals would find the games distasteful, but this is not always the case. While some writers and philosophers saw the gladiators and those who sponsored them as professional murderers, others could not help appreciating their courage and skill. Seneca the Elder (*c.* 55 BC–AD 39) appreciated their artistry while condemning the culture in which they flourished and Cicero (106–43 BC), though critical, could still admire them:

> Look at gladiators who are either ruined men or barbarians; what blows they endure! How is it that men, who have been well trained, prefer to receive a blow than basely avoid it? How frequently it is made evident that there is nothing they put higher than giving satisfaction to their owner or to the people! Even when weakened with wounds, they send word to their owners to ascertain their pleasure; if they have given satisfaction to them they are content to fall. What gladiator of ordinary merit has ever uttered a groan or changed countenance? Who of them has disgraced himself, I will not say on his feet, but who has disgraced himself in his fall? Who after falling has drawn in his neck when ordered to suffer the fatal stroke? A gladiatorial show is apt to seem cruel and brutal to some eyes, and I incline to think that as now conducted it is so. But in the days when it was criminals who crossed swords in the death struggle, there could be no better schooling against pain and death at any rate for the eye, though for the ear perhaps there might be many.

The twentieth century will probably be remembered as the most violent period ever: two world wars, the Russian Revolution and its aftermath, the Holocaust – genocide perpetrated on an unimaginable, unprecedented scale, not only in Europe but also in Africa and the Far East. The only real difference is that the Romans openly and without a shred of hypocrisy organized deliberate acts of violence for their own entertainment and built arenas specifically for the purpose. If people today were honest many would admit that the effect the gladiatorial contests had on Alypius, the Christian friend of St Augustine of Hippo (AD 354–430), might also apply to them. St Augustine offers the following anecdote in his *Confessions*:

He [Alypius] had gone to Rome before me in order to study law, and in Rome he had been quite swept away, incredibly and with a most incredible passion, by the gladiatorial shows. He was opposed to such things and detested them; but he happened to meet some of his friends and fellow students on their way back from lunch, and they, in spite of his protests and his vigorous resistance, used a friendly kind of violence and forced him to go along with them to the amphitheatre on a day when one of those cruel and bloody shows was being presented. As he went, he said to them: 'You can drag my body there, but don't imagine that you can make me turn my eyes or give my mind to the show. Though there, I shall not be there, and so I shall have the better of both of you and of the show.'

After hearing this his friends were all the keener to bring him along with them. No doubt they wanted to see whether he could do this or not. So they came to the arena and took what seats they could find. The whole place was seething with savage enthusiasm, but he shut his eyes and forbade his soul to go into a scene of such evil. If only he could have blocked up his ears too! For in the course of the fight some man fell; there was a great roar from the whole mass of the spectators which fell on his ears; he was overcome by curiosity and opened his eyes, feeling perfectly prepared to treat whatever he might see with scorn and to rise above it.

But he then received in his soul a worse wound than that man, whom he had wanted to see, had received on his body. His own fall was more wretched than that of the gladiator which had caused all that shouting which had entered his ears and unlocked his eyes and made an opening for the thrust that was to overthrow his soul – a soul that had been reckless rather than strong and was all the weaker because it had trusted in itself when it ought to have trusted in you. He saw the blood and gulped down savagery. Far from turning away, he fixed his eyes on it. Without knowing what was happening, he drank in madness, he was delighted with the guilty contest, drunk with the lust for blood. He was no longer the man who had come there but was one of the crowd to which he had come, a true companion of those who had brought him.

There is no more to be said. He looked, he shouted, he raved with excitement. He took away with him a madness which would goad him to come back again, and he would not only go with those who first got him there; he would go ahead of them and he would drag others with him ...

THE ANCIENT ROMANS

Today, if you stand on the Palatine Hill, where the Roman emperors built their palaces, and look towards the Arch of Titus and the Colosseum, it is difficult to imagine how the area must have appeared at the dawn of history. What would it have looked like to Romulus, the mythological founder of Rome, in 753 BC? His view would have been partially obscured by the Velian Hill, which has long since been flattened, but where the Colosseum now stands he would have seen an open area of marshland surrounded by a range of low hills.

Opposite
The Colosseum seen from the Palatine Hill. The columns of the Temple of Venus and Roma are in the foreground.

In the area where the Colosseum now stands, in a region known as Latium, a small stream flowed westwards down the broad Labican valley, which was flanked on the north and south by two of Rome's famous seven hills – the Esquiline and the Caelian respectively. Finding its course blocked by the Palatine and its northern spur, the Velian Hill, the stream was diverted southwards between the Caelian and Palatine. It then joined another stream and flowed along the southern edge of the Palatine to reach the River Tiber. The broad, low-lying flood-plain, where the Labican Stream turned south, was the catchment area for several rivulets trickling down the hills, and it was on the hills overlooking this marsh that the city of Rome was established.

The urban development of Rome was a slow process that began in the late Bronze Age, in about 1000 BC. Archaeological evidence, including burial remains, suggests that there were a few small settlements of thatched huts on the Palatine and neighbouring hills at this time. By the early Iron Age there was a substantial population living there, with further development northwards in the Forum Valley and on the Quirinal Hill. These settlements occupied a strategic position in relation to the River Tiber, which formed a natural border on an important route between the regions of Etruria to the north and Campania to the south. The description *pontifex maximus* (chief bridge-builder), a post originally held by the head priest of the city of Rome and a title subsequently adopted first by the emperors and then, from the beginning of the Christian era, all the popes, underlines the point.

While the hilltop villages continued to grow, an urban population began to colonize the valleys, as the town planners and engineers decided to drain and reclaim the marshlands. Early inscriptions indicate Rome's Latin origins but the Etruscan influence on the city, particularly in the religious sphere, was also substantial. There had been other incursions, too – from the Sabine hill tribes to the east (reflected in the legend of the rape of the Sabine women) and from Greek colonists to the south.

For about a hundred years, from around 616 BC, Rome came under Etruscan domination and the region was ruled by three elected kings. The first was an Etruscan, Tarquinius Priscus. He was succeeded by his son-in-law Servius Tullius, who was a Latin, and he was followed by Tarquinius Superbus (Tarquin the Proud), who was either the son or the grandson of Tarquinius Priscus – these rulers are semi-legendary and what little is known about them comes mainly from the Roman historian Livy (59 BC–AD 17).

In 510 BC Tarquinius Superbus was deposed and expelled from the city by a group of Roman aristocrats following a scandal involving his son Sextus, who raped a woman named Lucretia (an incident that has since stirred the imagination of many an artist looking for an ancient classical subject with erotic overtones). With his supporters, among them Lars Porsenna, Tarquinius Superbus tried to retake Rome several times, and may have succeeded, briefly, but he was repelled for the last time after a Latin victory at Aricia in 506 BC.

Etruscan rule was over but a process of urban and civic development had begun that the Romans would continue for the next thousand years. By the time they were driven out of Rome the invaders had left behind the concept of the city-state and had built the following: stone houses with tiled roofs; a system of paved roads; a main sewer, the Cloaca Maxima, which was fed by a network of underground drains coming down from the hills; the Pons Sublicus, which was the first bridge over the Tiber; the Forum Romanum, a city-centre market place devoted to commerce and politics; and several places of worship, including the Temple of Jupiter Capitolinus on the Capitol, which was the largest building in Italy at the time. They probably also left behind a race track of some kind for chariot-racing. Strangely, though they taught the Romans how to write, with a modified form of alphabet borrowed from the Greeks, they never passed on their language. Etruscan died out and is an intriguing linguistic anomaly for it seems not to be related to any other known language, while Latin flourished as the root of several dialects that eventually became modern Italian, Spanish, Portuguese, Romanian and French.

THE ROMAN REPUBLIC (509–27 BC)

After the Etruscans had been driven out the Romans decided that they had had enough of the monarchy and settled on a system of oligarchy instead. Headed by Lucius Junius Brutus, members of the ruling class (the patricians) created a Senate and from that body they elected two magistrates, later known as consuls, to see to the hands-on business of running things for a year at a time. It was a form of government that was always evolving, gradually becoming more democratic as the common people (the plebeians) demanded more civil rights. The plebeians eventually won the right to elect their own representatives, known as tribunes.

The fifth century BC was a period of cautious colonial expansion as the Romans defended themselves against neighbouring territories on the Italian peninsula. They were defeated many times but Roman tenacity finally won through. They suffered a setback in 394 BC when they found themselves under attack from the Gauls, who were gradually working their way southwards from central Europe. The Gauls succeeded in sacking Rome in 390, though they did not occupy the city. The city responded by strengthening its defences.

Rome's next powerful enemies were the Samnites, a group of Oscan-speaking hill tribes with whom they fought a series of protracted wars on and off between 343 and 290 BC. Their final victory meant that the Romans now had overall coast-to-coast control of a huge area of central and southern Italy that included the important cities of Beneventum (Benevento), Capua and Neapolis (Naples).

Expansion southwards continued unabated into the third century BC as Rome finally brought the Greek colonies of southern Italy into the fold. This was not achieved without a struggle. In 280 BC the maverick warlord Pyrrhus of Epirus landed in Italy with a Macedonian-style army of 25,000 men armed with pikes, and 20 elephants, and defeated the Romans, first at Heraclea and then the following year at Ausculum, suffering heavy losses of men both times. Reinforced by Rome's old enemies, the Samnites, he advanced to within 40 miles of Rome. He tried to negotiate with the Romans but they refused to deal with him. The Greek philosopher Plutarch (AD *c.* 46–*c.* 120) claims that Pyrrhus offered a bribe to a Roman ambassador, Fabricius, in an effort to get his enemy to listen to his peace plans and when this failed tried to intimidate him with one of his elephants. 'Your gold did not move me yesterday,' said the noble Fabricius, 'nor does your beast today.' Pyrrhus's elephants were the first the Romans had ever seen and they jokingly referred to them as 'Lucanian cows'.

It is a measure of the Romans' tenacity that while Pyrrhus and his sup-posedly superior army defeated them not once but twice, 'liberating' the whole of southern Italy in the process, he was still forced to retreat. Two costly victories for no gain. He returned in 275 BC and this time the Romans defeated him, in the Battle of Beneventum. The poor man has left his name to posterity in the shape of 'pyrrhic victories' – gains that have been won at such cost that they are perceived as disasters for the victor.

With southern Italy now under control, the Romans sought to complete their domination and in 264 BC the Roman legions crossed the Straits of Messina and landed in Sicily. They now embarked on the bloodiest conflict in their history – the Punic Wars.

Carthage was the great naval power of the western Mediterranean, with a trading empire that included Sardinia, western Sicily, North Africa and southeastern Spain. Rome entered this conflict as a little-known power, totally insignificant compared to either Carthage or the eastern Mediterranean super-powers – Macedonia, Syria and Egypt – that had emerged after the death of Alexander the Great in 323 BC.

The first of the Punic Wars against Carthage lasted from 264 to 241 BC and Roman victories gave them control of

Sicily and Sardinia. It had also turned them into a formidable naval power. The Carthaginians then concentrated their efforts on Spain, building up a power base from which the legendary general Hannibal was able to invade Italy in 218. He was finally defeated in 201, by which time Rome had eclipsed all the other great powers. Philip V of Macedon was defeated at Cynoscephalae in Thessaly in 197, Antiochus the Great of Syria was toppled at Magnesia seven years later, and the kings of Egypt became vassals.

The eminent scholar John Mann once described Rome's political system as a desperate attempt to keep up with the incredible success of its army. Before the Punic Wars ordinary Roman citizens were just beginning to enjoy a certain level of democracy, but the continuing conflict with Carthage led to a less stable society and an erosion of civil rights and privileges as a wider gulf developed between the upper and lower classes. By the end of the third century the state was controlled by a few powerful noble families who formed the Senate. Rome had originally confined its military activity to defending itself against its neighbours on the Italian peninsula, such as the Aequi and the Volsci, and it had done this with an army consisting largely of farm workers. These men were conscripted on a rota system in the spring, after the crops had been sown, and then demobilized in late summer, in time to bring the harvest in. The Punic Wars changed all that. Many men left the land to become professional soldiers. They were sent far away from home and often did not return for several years. Sometimes they never came back. As a consequence, if there were no men left behind to work the land, farms were abandoned and whole families moved to the city. The attraction was that Rome operated a primitive welfare system and gave basic food rations to those who were unable to support themselves.

The migration of people from the countryside to the capital continued as a new development hit the traditional rural economy. As the empire expanded, small farms became unprofitable because more and more of them were taken over and turned into huge agricultural estates to be worked by slaves. And the slave population continued to grow as the Romans conquered one territory after another and shipped their captives back to Italy. Putting them to work on the land was one way of dealing with them. Turning them into gladiators was another.

Most of the indigenous people who settled in Rome, therefore, were from peasant stock. They were used to hardship but were often on the edge of starvation. It was a volatile population, prone to revolt. The ruling elite's solution was, in Juvenal's memorable phrase, 'bread and circuses' – basic food and entertainment – a strategy designed to keep the plebs from expressing their dissatisfaction too violently. The gladiatorial games formed part of this popular strategy of appeasing the populace with public events.

During the first century BC, as Rome extended its influence ever further – from the Rhine and the Danube in central Europe to the Euphrates and the Nile in North Africa, from the Iberian peninsula in the west to Armenia in the east – the civilization reached its apogee. It was the era of writers and poets such as Virgil, Cicero, Horace, Sallust and Livy, whose wonderful classic works tell us so much about Rome, the Romans and their history. The downside, unfortunately, was that this was also a period of unremitting civil strife. The relatively enlightened political

system that had worked so well when Rome was a tight-knit and self-contained city-state was less well suited to the demands and commitments of a sprawling empire.

The balance of power that had previously characterized the relationship between the tribunes and the senate began to break down as the power base shifted to the military commanders. These tough warlords were the new Roman heroes and it was they who exploited the weaknesses of the political system, playing one group off against the other. The names of many of these generals are known – Marius, Sulla, Pompey, Julius Caesar, Crassus, Mark Antony – because they shaped the Roman world.

The Forum seen from the Capitol with the Colosseum in the background.

JULIUS CAESAR AND THE FIRST TRIUMVIRATE

Julius Caesar (100–44 BC) was a great general, a great statesman and a great impresario. For his multiple triumph in 46 BC he imported six hundred lions, four hundred other large cats, 20 elephants and a rhinoceros and held a huge animal hunt. He is said to have sent 1500 men, one third of them mounted, and 40 elephants into the arena to do battle in two separate events.

His capacity for conspicuous extravagance had hardly grown since he held his first spectacle in 65 BC, when he put on a massive show involving 320 pairs of gladiators armed with silver weapons. They were pitted against each other in combat and also against a series of wild animals. In tune with the custom of the day he claimed the event was intended to honour his father. The valediction was a pretext, of course, for his father was long since dead. At this stage of his political career Caesar was just another ambitious young magistrate looking for popular support. This habit of holding a *munus* to win over the crowds at election time, together with the bribery that often went along with it, was becoming such a serious problem that the Senate eventually passed a law in 63 BC banning all games during the two years preceding an election.

Caesar had plotted his career carefully, having forged an alliance with two rich and powerful men, Pompey and Crassus, in 60 BC, in order to gain more influence over the Senate. This coalition, known as the First Triumvirate, was further cemented when Pompey married Caesar's daughter Julia. With such influential allies, Caesar's appointment as consul in 59 BC came as a matter of course, but he had also made some powerful enemies. As he rose to prominence he began to employ gladiators as personal bodyguards. Under the command of an aristocratic bully named Clodius, these men were thugs, basically. While Caesar was away fighting the Gallic wars and invading Britain, Clodius and his henchmen were conducting their own reign of terror, forcing Pompey's ally Cicero into exile and physically attacking Pompey himself. It is reported that Pompey was brought home injured and covered in blood; Julia, who was heavily pregnant at the time, went into labour and died in childbirth. Pompey retaliated by forming his own band of thugs, controlled by a man called Milo. Milo's gang included two well-known gladiators, Eudamus and Birria. The two groups clashed one day and Clodius was killed. His supporters brought his body along the Appian Way into Rome and he was cremated on a magnificent

Julius Caesar held his first spectacle in Rome in 65 BC and had a reputation for extravagance.

funeral pyre. Accused of his murder, Milo went into exile at Marseilles.

Julia's death served to widen the rift between Caesar and Pompey (Crassus was dead by then, killed in battle in 53 BC) and by the time Caesar returned to Italy in 50 the two men had ended up on different sides of the civil war that had broken out. Cicero reports that at this stage Caesar had control of five thousand gladiators based in the barracks at Capua. Pompey seized them, disarmed them and dispersed them by billeting them in pairs on his supporters. The civil war continued until 45 BC, by which time Pompey had been killed in battle (in 48 BC) and Caesar had held three triumphs to celebrate his victories in Gaul and elsewhere. These involved some lavish games, as the Roman historian Suetonius (AD *c.* 69–*c.* 150) records:

> He gave entertainments of diverse kinds: a combat of gladiators and also stage plays in every ward of the city ... as well as races in the circus, athletic contests ... combats with wild beasts were presented on five successive days and last of all there was a battle between two opposing armies in which five hundred infantry, 20 elephants and 30 horsemen engaged on each side ... For the naval battle a pool was dug in the lesser Codeta [a swampy area on the Campus Martius, next to the Tiber] and there was a contest of ships ...

The animal hunts involved four hundred lions and, for the very first time in Rome, several giraffes. Caesar's mock naval battle (*naumachia*) on this occasion is the first recorded in the capital. It involved four thousand oarsmen and two thousand warriors, in costume, re-enacting an historical encounter between the Phoenicians and the Egyptians. These events were so crowded, that several people were crushed to death, including two senators.

Two years later Caesar was assassinated, the result of a coup against him led by Cassius, a general, and a fellow senator, Brutus. Civil war broke out again and peace was only restored with the defeat of Mark Antony and Caesar's ex-mistress Cleopatra at the Battle of Actium in 31 BC.

THE ROMAN EMPIRE (27 BC–AD 476)

Just as we know of the powerful generals who seized power in Rome so we have all heard of the emperors who succeeded them. These rulers were omnipotent. Most of them were ruthless and some of them were quite simply mad as well. The first five Roman emperors, who between them ruled for nearly a century, from 31 BC to AD 68, were Augustus, Tiberius, Caligula, Claudius and Nero, and together formed what came to be known as the Julio-Claudian dynasty.

AUGUSTUS

Julius Caesar's adopted son Octavian, known later as Augustus, had emerged as the undisputed first ruler of the Roman Empire in 31 BC after the period of civil strife that marked the end of the Republican era. He enjoyed a long reign, during which time he created a relatively stable society and gained the trust of the Senate and the people. He scaled down the military, created bodies to take charge of policing the streets and fire-watching, and reformed the system of currency. He taxed the people prudently and spent the money on improving the conditions of the ordinary citizen. He did not seek to enrich himself but concentrated on civic improvements, such as the completion of the Theatre of Marcellus in 11 BC (named in honour of his nephew), and a new Forum that was finished in 2 BC. His claim for Rome that he 'found it brick and left it marble' is more than justified.

Rome, by then with a population of around a million, was growing as a trading centre and was about to overtake Alexandria as the hub of the civilized world. His was a golden age, the age of Horace, Virgil and Livy, and Augustus made sure that art and literature flourished under his patronage. (He made an example of the poet Ovid, however, and sent him into exile in AD 8 because he felt he was not reverential enough.) Not that his interests were exclusively cerebral. He is said to have sent ten thousand gladiators into the arena and Suetonius declared that he 'surpassed all his predecessors in the frequency, variety and magnificence of his public shows'. But he recognized that the games were open to political abuse and in 22 BC he passed a law limiting the praetors (magistrates ranking on the next level below a consul) to two shows while in office, with a maximum of 120 gladiators.

Roman coin bearing the likeness of Augustus.

The games were now a regular feature of Roman life and the most important one was always held to coincide with the festival of Saturnalia, which was held at the winter solstice in honour of Saturn, the god identified with crops and agriculture. Augustus was responsible for establishing the tradition of holding the animal hunts (*venationes*) in the mornings, the executions at midday and the gladiatorial contests (*munera*) in the afternoons. He also decreed that a losing gladiator should not automatically be killed but would have his fate decided by the public, with the emperor having the final say.

OCEANUS
(Atlantic Ocean)

BRITANNIA

GERMANIA

GAUL
(Gallia)

GAUL (Gallia Cisalpina)

DACIA

PONTUS EUXINUS
(Black Sea)

ILLYRICUM

HISPANIA

CORSICA

ITALY

ROME

SARDINIA

THRACIA

MARE INTERNUM

ASIA

MAURETANIA

SICILIA

ACHAIA

(Mediterranean Sea)

SYRIA

AFRICA

CYRENAICA

TIBERIUS

Tiberius was Augustus's adopted son and nominated successor but had not been his first choice. Maybe at the age of 54 Tiberius was too old to settle happily into the role of emperor and all the other offices that came with the job, for he was not a natural statesman and had spent most of his working life in the army, serving in the Rhineland and the Balkans. His reign is generally considered to have been undistinguished, marked by a lack of interest in public life. He commissioned very few new buildings and did not relish the gladiatorial games.

The Roman historian Tacitus (AD *c*. 56–*c*. 120) records a disaster that happened in a wooden amphitheatre during his reign (AD 14–37), when 50,000 people were killed or injured:

Roman coin bearing the likeness of Tiberius.

> Atilius, the son of a freedman, undertook to build an amphitheatre at Fidenae for the exhibition of gladiators. The foundation was inadequate and the superstructure insufficiently braced ... the place being at no great distance from Rome, a vast conflux of men and women, old and young, crowded together. The consequence was that the building, overloaded with spectators, gave way at once. All who were inside, besides a prodigious multitude that stood round the place were crushed under the ruins. The condition of those who perished instantly was the happiest. They escaped the pangs of death, while the maimed and lacerated lingered in torment, beholding as long as daylight lasted, their wives and children in equal agony, and, during the night, pierced to the heart by their shrieks and groans.

In spite of this catastrophe Tiberius made no attempt to ban wooden amphitheatres. Instead Atilius was blamed for not spending enough money on building the amphitheatre properly and he was banished. Such buildings continued to go up and they occasionally collapsed. Over a thousand people were killed in an amphitheatre disaster in the middle of the second century AD and there was another one a century and a half later.

CALIGULA

The whole of Caligula's short life was one of political intrigue. He was barely in his twenties when his mother and two of his brothers were

Opposite
The Roman empire in AD 80 stretched from Spain to Syria and from England to Egypt.

executed amid accusations of conspiracy to kill Tiberius, who was his great-uncle. His brief reign began in AD 37 and ended violently with his assassination during a gladiatorial show outside the imperial palace on the Palatine Hill in AD 41. He was 29 years old. He emerges from the various descriptions of him as a neurotic insomniac, an ugly man greedy for gold, jewels and other riches, and capable of extreme cruelty born of envy and insecurity.

Suetonius tells us that Caligula was the first emperor to become really enthusiastic about chariot-racing, gladiators and the games. He supported the Thracians – he sometimes appeared in the arena dressed as one himself and he placed two of them in command of his bodyguards – and he hated their traditional opponents, the *murmillones*. Men from both groups engaged in mock fights with him, using wooden swords. There was one occasion when Caligula was practising with a *murmillo* who feigned a fall rather too realistically. The emperor stabbed him with a dagger and then ran about the arena waving a palm branch, just as the real victors did.

Roman bust of Caligula, who found the perfect outlet for his sadism in the arena.

When it came to the games, he took every opportunity to show his subjects just how sadistic he could be. He loved to humiliate people in public and the Colosseum seemed like an excellent place to do this. It gave him pleasure to pitch a feeble old man against a fit young criminal in the arena and he would often force disabled people to dress up as *paegniarii* – the clowns and comic actors of the gladiatorial world. On hot days he would have the awning taken down, refuse to let anyone leave, and then watch people suffering in the baking sun.

Caligula was jealous of the good looks of Aesius Proculus, nicknamed the Giant Cupid, and the son of a top centurion. Caligula ordered him to be dragged into the arena and matched first against a *retiarius* and then a *secutor*. When Proculus won both fights Caligula had him dragged through the streets in rags and executed. His greed knew no bounds. He insisted that his subjects should will their property to him and sold off anything that came into his possession. Once when he was selling gladiators he noticed that senator Aponius Saturninus had nodded off. He told the auctioneer to accept the sleeping senator's nods as bids, with the result that Saturninus awoke to find he had bought 13 gladiators and owed the emperor 9 million sesterces.

Tiberius had found the games rather boring and had tried to restrict them but Caligula was much more hands-on. He created the special post of *curator munerum*, a sort of events organizer, but killed the first man to take the job. What this man's offence was is not recorded but Suetonius says that Caligula had him 'beaten with chains in his presence for several successive days, and only killed him when he became disgusted at the stench of his putrefied brain'.

CLAUDIUS

The popular image of Caligula's uncle Claudius comes from Robert Graves's two novels, *I, Claudius* and *Claudius the God*, written in the 1930s and dramatized for British television in the 1970s. Presented as though they were genuine autobiographies, these fictional accounts create the image of an intelligent, sensitive man, handicapped by spasmodic movements and a stammer, who turns into a tyrant and is betrayed by those closest to him. His growing paranoia was perhaps justified as he was the victim of several assassination attempts,

Roman bust of Claudius.

and his death in AD 54 was certainly suspicious. There were rumours that his wife Agrippina had poisoned him. She was to die a violent death herself five years later, at the hands of her own son, Nero, who had ordered her assassination. She reportedly confronted the centurion who had been sent to kill her with the words, 'Here, strike the womb that bore a monster.'

NERO

In AD 57 Nero had a richly decorated wooden amphitheatre built on the Campus Martius, a site he chose because the arena could be flooded with water from the nearby River Tiber to put on naval battles and sea monster shows. Somewhat uncharacteristically, Nero went for a bloodless inauguration for his amphitheatre and did not even bother with the usual midday executions, though he took the opportunity to humiliate four hundred senators and six hundred equestrians by compelling them to take part in a mock gladiator contest and an animal hunt.

The Golden Palace

In AD 64 Nero's amphitheatre and the Theatre of Taurus were both destroyed in a fire that swept through the area to the east of the Palatine Hill, where the imperial palace was situated. Thousands of people were made homeless and the angry mob pointed the finger at their emperor, claiming that he had done nothing to help them. This is the origin of the story that Nero fiddled while Rome burned (he was an accomplished lyre-player). Whatever he was doing at the time, Nero swiftly passed the buck by blaming the Christians and making an example of some of them by having them executed. And then, like all good despots, he continued to ignore the plight of his people and decided instead to put the razed land to good use by refurbishing his old palace.

Nero's new residence, the Golden Palace (Domus Aurea), and its landscaped estate covered an area of about 125 acres. The original site on the Palatine Hill was extended across the valleys and hills to the east and north as far as the old walls of the city and included lavish accommodation beside an artificial ornamental lake, surrounded by vineyards, woodland and animal pastures.

By this time Nero had surrounded himself with servile admirers who encouraged his grandiose schemes and shielded him from the city's problems. He preferred to spend his time studying poetry, drama and music.

Paranoia gradually took hold of him and he began to think that everyone was plotting against him. He suspected conspiracy at every turn, especially among the aristocracy, whom he had always mistrusted, and he ordered the execution without trial of several senators. This act turned his fears into a self-fulfilling prophecy and he was soon aware of a genuine plot to get rid of him. More executions followed. The Senate declared Nero a public enemy and offered the throne to Galba, the governor of Spain. Nero now had nowhere to go. The Praetorian Guard turned against him and he tried to flee the city but found all escape routes blocked. He took the only honourable way left open to him: he plunged a dagger into his heart and killed himself.

Roman coin bearing the likeness of Nero, whose Golden Palace stood on the site subsequently occupied by the Colosseum.

VESPASIAN

Emperor Vespasian, unlike Nero, was not a nobleman but a member of the equestrian class (the class below the senatorial class) and he had worked his way up through the system. As was common at the time, his military and political careers progressed in parallel. He was elected a military tribune at the age of 18 and then became a quaestor (the lowest rank of magistrate). By the age of 31 he had achieved the rank of aedile (a junior magistrate in charge of public works) and was then made a praetor (the second to highest level of magistrate).

Vespasian served in Thrace (modern Bulgaria) and Crete and in AD 42 Claudius made him the commander of a legion and sent him to Strasbourg, moving him to Britain a year later, where he took part in the capture of Camulodunum (Colchester). He received honours during Claudius's triumph in AD 44 and returned to Rome three years later. He became a consul in AD 51 but for ten years the political intrigue involving Claudius's fourth wife, Agrippina, and her son Nero deprived Vespasian of the governorship to which he felt he was entitled. Whenever his detractors wanted to insult him they would call him 'the mule-trader' – a reference to the way he made a living during these lean years without imperial patronage.

Claudius's death cleared the way for Vespasian to return to public life and he was rewarded with the governorship he had waited so long for and sent to North Africa. He was regarded as a just and honourable governor if

not a particularly popular one, though at least he did not use the position to increase his own personal wealth. He was with Nero on a tour of Greece when news came through of a revolt in Jerusalem. Nero gave him the job of putting down the revolt. He set out for Judaea, travelling overland through Turkey, while his son Titus, who was 27, was despatched by sea to Alexandria. In March AD 67 Vespasian reached Antioch in Syria, where he joined forces with Titus to advance into Galilee and Samaria. One by one the cities, towns and mountain strongholds succumbed to the Roman onslaught – Gabara, Jotapata, Tiberias, Tarichae, Gamala – and Vespasian marched southwards towards Jericho, knocking out all the key towns on the route to Jerusalem.

Vespasian was in Caesarea when he heard of Nero's death and the succession of the new emperor, Galba. It was soon obvious that this appointment was not at all popular and there were some legions, most notably those serving in northern Germany, who had refused to swear allegiance to him. They had wanted their own commander, Verginius, to be emperor. Galba swiftly recalled Verginius to Rome to forestall any revolt but failed to win the Senate round. As a result Rome went through a brief period of civil unrest and between AD 68 and 69 suffered three emperors altogether – Galba (assassinated), Otho (committed suicide) and Vitellius (assassinated).

Vespasian emerged victorious from this bloodbath and his ten-year reign from AD 69 marked the start of a new dynasty and a reformed system of imperial rule. It was a period of peace and stability and Vespasian placed the emphasis on building public rather than private memorials. He was determined to win the people's respect and one of his more popular gestures was to throw the gardens of Nero's Golden Palace open to the public. He also started to develop the idea of building a permanent amphitheatre there.

Opposite
Roman bust of Vespasian, who commissioned the building of the Colosseum in AD 69. He would not live to see its completion.

VESPASIAN'S VISION

When Vespasian embarked on his grand plan for the Colosseum he was trying to do something that no one had ever attempted before: to build an all-purpose, permanent, stone amphitheatre that would be the greatest entertainment venue in the world. On becoming emperor in AD 69 he had adopted the motto *Roma Resurgens* – 'Rome rises from the ashes'. This was a direct reference to the fire that had destroyed so much of the city during Nero's reign five years earlier, and Vespasian was determined to start his programme of regeneration with something impressive.

Opposite
An impression of how the Colosseum would have appeared in the early second century.

To be absolutely correct we should refer to the Colosseum as the Amphitheatrum Flavium, which is a reference to Flavius, Vespasian's family name. The word 'Colosseum' is probably medieval and the first citation appears in a traditional saying, 'When falls the Colosseum, Rome shall fall', quoted by the Venerable Bede in the eighth century AD. Popular belief holds that this is a reference to the Colossus Neronis, a huge statue of Nero that once stood near the Colosseum on the northwestern side, but most scholars doubt this, preferring the rather more prosaic explanation that, like the Colossus of Rhodes, it was the enormous structure itself that gave rise to the name.

Most of the historical information concerning the Colosseum in its topographical and historical setting comes down to us from Martial (AD *c*. 40–*c*. 104), the poet laureate of his day. His book of epigrams, *De Spectaculis*, celebrates the inauguration of the Colosseum in AD 80, and although his style is perhaps too ornate and his descriptions a bit overblown for modern taste, he was actually there and so we have the luxury of an account from a genuine eyewitness:

> Where the starry Colossus sees the constellations at close range and lofty scaffolding rises in the middle of the road, once gleamed the odious halls of a cruel monarch, and in all Rome there stood a single house. Where rises before our eyes the noble structure of the Amphitheatre, was once Nero's lake. Where we admire the warm baths, a speedy gift, a haughty tract of land had robbed the poor of their dwellings.

The cruel monarch that Martial refers to is Nero, the 'single house' is his Golden Palace, and the 'warm baths' are the Baths of Titus. These baths, which Vespasian's son Titus had built on the site of the old imperial palace, were connected to the Colosseum piazza by a stone staircase.

Vespasian had told his architects that he wanted the very best in backstage facilities, featuring special enclosures for wild animals and a sophisticated system of lifts and trapdoors designed to get them and the scenery and props quickly up into the arena. The Roman crowds loved the spectacle of combat in all its forms – gladiatorial contests, animal fights and sea-battles – and Vespasian wanted to give them something really sen-sational. Nero had put on some impressive shows, as had the others of the Julio-Claudian dynasty, but they had had to make do with various makeshift theatres down by the Tiber and the Circus Maximus, which was primarily a racetrack not really suitable for gladiatorial combat. Vespasian had a much grander vision.

THE CIRCUS MAXIMUS

The Circus Maximus, situated in the broad valley between the Palatine and Aventine Hills, was the oldest entertainment venue in Rome. According to legend the area was first developed for chariot-racing during the reign of Tarquinius Priscus in the sixth century BC. This date fits in with the chariot races that are sometimes depicted on Etruscan tombs and burial urns of the same period. The Circus was often waterlogged because it was situated on marshland and the Roman historian Livy (59 BC–AD 17) records that the Tiber burst its banks and flooded the course at a time when races were taking place there one day in 363 BC. After this the land was drained several times and, according to Livy, wooden spectator stands were put up.

The remains of the Circus Maximus can clearly be seen in the foreground of this aerial photograph with the Palatine Hill and the Colosseum behind.

These stood some 4 metres off the ground, to improve visibility. Starting gates were installed in 329 BC.

The Circus Maximus began to acquire a more formal appearance during the second century BC, by which time it was a regular venue for animal hunts. Iron railings were put up around the racetrack to protect the public and it is recorded that there was an occasion during one of Pompey's shows when the elephants tried to break through them. The permanent central division of the track was probably constructed in around 174 BC.

Nobody bothered much about controlling how the Circus developed until the middle of the first century BC, when Julius Caesar decided it needed a facelift and went for an elongated U-shaped stadium. Augustus continued the refurbishment but work was interrupted by a fire in 31 BC. In its final form the Circus was 600 metres long and 200 metres wide and capable of seating an estimated 250,000 people, five times the capacity of the Colosseum. The racetrack itself, by far the largest in the Roman world, was about 540 metres long and 80 metres wide.

Archaeologists have established that the rebuilt Circus Maximus was constructed according to the same design of superimposed barrel vaults as many other entertainment venues in Rome of the time. It was on the route of the triumphal processions that used to start off at the south side of the Capitol and pass round the Palatine Hill and end at the Forum, and in AD 81 a triumphal arch dedicated to Titus was built into the seating area at the eastern end.

There were two other smaller circuses in Rome performing a similar function to the Circus Maximus: the Circus Flaminius and the Stadium of Domitian, both in the Campus Martius (Field of Mars), an area of marshland down by the River Tiber, to the west of the city, beyond the old Servian Wall. No trace of the Circus Flaminius remains but, although unexcavated, the shape of Domitian's stadium is preserved in the Piazza Navona.

THE EARLY AMPHITHEATRES

When it was finished, the Colosseum was 52 metres high and ran for 188 metres along its long axis and 156 metres along its short axis. The arena covered an area of 3,357 square metres and the seating capacity was around

The amphitheatre
at Pompeii.

50,000. It remained the largest and the most complex amphitheatre in the
ancient world. Its architectural style and method of construction set the
standard for similar buildings throughout the Roman Empire, though none
of them was ever quite so ambitious. There are only two other amphitheatres that could be said to have been in the same league, both of them
built in the second century AD in southern Italy: Capua (Santa Maria
Capua Vetere) and Puteoli (Pozzuoli). There are other significant but less
grand examples at Verona in Italy, Emerita Augusta (Mérida), Italica and
Tarraco (Tarragona) in Spain, Nemausus (Nîmes) in France and Thysdrus
(El Djem) in Tunisia.

The earliest amphitheatres for which there is archaeological evidence
were in Campania in southwestern Italy. It has been established that three
of these, which were on the same sites as later amphitheatres at Capua,
Cumae and Liternum, date from the end of the second century BC. The
remains are not substantial enough to allow a reconstruction to their
original plan. A further four important examples from the same region – at
Atella, Cales, Telese and Pompeii – can be dated to the first half of the
first century BC.

The amphitheatre at Pompeii survives almost intact. Built in about
70 BC, it is an unpretentious structure sunk into a specially excavated pit.
The terraces are set into an embankment, enclosed by the city walls on the

Seating for the amphitheatre at Sutri is hewn out of rock.

south and east sides and a retaining wall reinforced by 62 buttresses on the north and west sides. It is 135 metres long and 104 metres wide and the arena, which has no substructures beneath it, measures about 65 × 35 metres. The seating area (*cavea*), which had 35 rows of seats divided into three distinct levels, would have held about 20,000 people. The balustrade (*balteus*) between the podium and the arena is only just over 2 metres high so it would have offered the audience at the front very poor protection during the animal hunts.

Until this time all amphitheatres, whether they were modest or grand, had to be built into naturally sloping ground or created from excavated pits and man-made embankments so that the tiers of terraced seating could be fitted into the contours of the landscape. There are two especially fine examples of amphitheatres in a spectacular natural setting in Italy – one at Sutri, which was totally hewn out of rock, and one at Casino, which was built into a hillside. Most amphitheatres were fairly simple in construction, consisting of a basic oval arena with a banked seating area around it, usually constructed of wood on a masonry foundation. Most areas where people had settled had some form of venue that offered a performance space to itinerant gladiator troupes and other entertainers. The Romans believed in providing recreation facilities for its troops and most large established army bases would have had an amphitheatre of sorts. Those at Chester in England and Xanten in Germany are well known.

THEATRE OF POMPEY

In 55 BC Pompey had a theatre built on the Campus Martius. At this time all stone buildings intended as permanent places of entertainment were banned in Rome. This restriction seems to date back to the second century BC and stems from the traditional Roman view that secular theatres were immoral places invented by the Greeks. Many temples in Rome functioned like theatres, in fact, offering staged rituals in front of an audience as a form of worship, but as long as their purpose was religious they were acceptable. Pompey knew this but he wanted something better than the usual temporary wooden structures and he devised a clever way to get round the law. When the builders had finished the *cavea* he got them to stick a temple dedicated to Venus the Conqueror on top of it. The stone seating terraces looked like a suitably grand stairway leading up to a conventional place of worship. Pompey said the place was a sacred precinct and got away with it.

As well as being the biggest theatre in the world at that time, with a capacity estimated to have been around 17,600, the Theatre of Pompey was built to a completely revolutionary design. Greek theatres were always built into a hillside which could be used to support the seating. Only the stage and scenic areas were freestanding. The invention of concrete made it possible for the Romans to build totally freestanding theatres, such as Pompey's. Though the seating system was copied from the Greeks, the *cavea* rested on a foundation of barrel vaults constructed in a pattern of radiating spokes from a central hub. This system created a network of tunnels underneath the seating area and these were used for access to the stadium and for storage. The Theatre of Pompey has never been properly excavated as it lies beneath an intensely built-up area to the northwest of the Capitol, but some parts of the concrete vaulting are visible in the basements of modern buildings.

Pompey's design was so ingenious that it quickly became a basic template for most theatres and amphitheatres elsewhere, including the Colosseum more than a hundred years later. Roman planners were now liberated from the constraints of landscape and were free to put their arenas on the flattest of flat plains and the wettest of wet marshes if they wished. They also realized that if they put two semicircles together to form a circle or ellipse they could cater for twice the number of people as before.

CURIO'S *SPECTACULA*

Scribonius Curio was a politician, and two years after the Theatre of Pompey was built he decided to put on a show lasting several days in honour of his father, who had died. He designed his own theatre specially for the occasion and as the ban on permanent entertainment venues was still in force he chose wood. Before the word 'amphitheatre' was adopted in around 2 BC the Romans used the term *spectacula*, meaning both the buildings and the shows that were put on there. Curio's design for his *spectacula* was certainly innovative for it involved not one but two separate semicircular theatres. Each had its own arena and seating area, which were connected and could be moved in tandem by means of a system of pivots through an angle of 180 degrees to form an ellipse. Curio kept the arenas apart in order to offer two alternative but simultaneous theatrical shows in the mornings and then pushed them together for the gladiatorial contests in the afternoons. According to the Roman statesman Pliny the Elder (AD 23-79), who describes this folly of a building in Book 36 of his encyclopaedic work *Natural History*, there was one day when Curio decided to carry out this manoeuvre while the audience were still in their seats:

> What will prove to be more amazing than anything is the madness of a people that was bold enough to take its place in such treacherous, rickety seats. Here we have a nation that has conquered the earth ... all swaying on a contraption ... When the earth yawns and cities are engulfed, whole communities grieve. Here the entire Roman people, as if on board two frail boats, was supported by a couple of pivots. They were entertained with the spectacle of risking life in the fighting arena, doomed as it were, to perish at some moment or other if the framework were wrenched out of place.

Apparently the revolving pivot mechanism jammed before the end of the games (the two theatres were pushed together as one at the time) and Curio was forced to reschedule the athletic displays he had planned for a grand finale on the last day. He went ahead and put the two shows on, one after the other, so his audience got double the entertainment. His venture got him into debt but Julius Caesar, who saw him as a useful political ally, is said to have bailed him out.

There are some scholars who say that Curio's building could never have got off the drawing board because builders at that time would not have had the technical know-how to make it work. Others believe that Pliny was trying to find an example to illustrate that the word 'amphitheatre', borrowed from the Greek and taken to mean 'double theatre', and so believed it had existed because it suited his theory. In spite of its stunning and revolutionary (in all senses of the word) design, no one else seems to have copied it and if it had ever been built it had certainly disappeared by the time Pliny came to write about it.

AMPHITHEATRE OF TAURUS

The Romans continued to build temporary wooden amphitheatres well into the second century AD, presumably because they were quicker and cheaper to put up than stone ones. These structures often collapsed or caught fire, of course, sometimes with fatal consequences.

There were inevitably some people who aspired to something more prestigious but if this was the case then they needed to be wealthy. One such was a man called Statilius Taurus, who built an amphitheatre in Rome in 29 BC. A description of this building, situated like the Theatre of Pompey on the Campus Martius, appears in the writings of Cassius Dio (AD 164–*fl.* AD 229), a Greek-born Roman senator and historian, who calls it a 'hunting theatre', which was quite a common appellation at the time. Very little is known about the Theatre of Taurus or the man who paid for it. Cassius Dio says that was destroyed in the fire of AD 64 but archaeologists have been unable to find any remains that would identify it.

BUILDING THE COLOSSEUM

The greatest task facing the builders of the Colosseum when work first started in AD 70 was to make sure that the foundations were strong enough to support such an enormous structure, especially as the proposed site was marshy. The principles of land drainage and stabilization were well understood by this time and Roman engineers had already altered the course of the Labican Stream, which flowed under the selected site, in order to incorporate it into their sewerage network. Nero had later had the stream channelled around the ornamental lake in the grounds of his Golden Palace. When the Colosseum was built, this diverted sewer ran along the south side of the building and joined the main drainage system that carried the city's effluent under the streets into the River Tiber.

DRAINAGE AND WATER SUPPLY

The drainage system serving the Colosseum was remarkably efficient and is a real tribute to the engineers who designed it. Conduits ran round the outside of the building, just beneath the paving of the piazza, and these collected part of the water, mainly rainwater, draining off the main seating area and the piazza itself. At regular intervals this drain discharged into

Above Three of
the building materials
used in the Colosseum:
travertine (left), concrete
(upper right) and brick
(lower right).

Above right Traces
of the housing for the
lead pipes of one of the
fountains on the first level
can be seen in this
travertine pillar.

a lower drain 8 metres beneath the piazza, connecting four large water conduits to the main drainage system. These were built onto the outside of the containing wall of the foundations, with sluices to control the flow.

Altogether there were nearly 3000 metres of water channels and tunnels serving the building. These included inflow and outflow pipes and the largest conduits probably served both purposes. The system of water channels which can be seen set into the brickwork of the highest level inside the Amphitheatre held lead pipes supplying the cisterns required for an internal water supply. Sadly there were no lead pipes to be found when the Colosseum was first excavated as these had been stripped away by looters very early on. Half these lead pipes would have been for the intake of water and the other half for its distribution around the building. The supply pipes could only have worked by a siphon system filtering water from a source at a higher level than the top floor of the Amphitheatre. The remains of eleven fountains have been identified on the first level of the Colosseum and their position allows us to speculate that there were probably another 17, making a total of 20 in the whole circuit. The remains of these fountains show that they were composed of three slabs of stone that formed a trough on the inside of the travertine pillars supporting the arches. Similar fountains with a spout are well known from excavations at Pompeii. (The drainage system is described in further detail in Appendix I.)

THE FOUNDATIONS

The technique of mixing and using concrete had been developed in Campania in southwest Italy during the third century BC. The Roman method was to lay courses of aggregate made up of leucite, an extremely solid and impermeable volcanic rock, fixed in place with layers of mortar made with volcanic sand (*pozzolana*). This material would set hard even in wet conditions and it allowed the Romans to construct vaulted buildings. City planners seized on the opportunity of building upwards, vault upon vault, and it was the method employed in building the Colosseum superstructure.

Once Vespasian had approved the location, size and general design of the Colosseum with his architects and before the engineers, demolition teams, craftsmen and labourers could start work, the quantity surveyors assessed the job and calculated exactly what materials would be needed. Their estimates were as follows: 100,000 cubic metres of hard travertine limestone; 300 tonnes of iron clamps to hold the stone blocks together; more than 250,000 cubic metres of mortar and aggregate to make the concrete; 1 million or so bricks of various sizes; and lesser amounts of soft tufa.

One of the stairwells leading from the third annular corridor. Travertine piers can be seen in the walls, left and right, with tufa surmounted by brickwork on either side.

Some of the materials were sourced locally – Rome already had many well-established brickworks, and tufa came from the crumbling old walls of the city – but much of it had to be brought into the city by ox cart. Hard travertine, for example, was quarried in Tivoli, some 35 kilometres away, and the marble came from northern Italy and various parts of the Roman Empire. Julius Caesar had prohibited the use of wheeled vehicles during daylight hours in an attempt to cut down the number of serious accidents they caused, but Vespasian suspended this edict so that the work on the Colosseum could continue day and night.

By this time Rome was used to producing large stone buildings and there were plenty of construction workers and artisans – draughtsmen, surveyors, vaulting engineers, drainage engineers, marble masons, travertine masons, tufa masons, bricklayers, iron-workers, carpenters, painters and sculptors – to do the job. These skilled men belonged to specialized guilds, which ensured a certain level of pay and decent conditions (and a proper burial when they died), but many of the demolition workers and labourers were slaves.

Before work could begin on the foundations, part of the colonnade along the western boundary of Nero's palace gardens had to be demolished and the ornamental lake drained. A vast trench was excavated, sinking 6 metres below the bottom of the lake to penetrate 4 metres into the clay subsoil. This trench was more than 50 metres wide and formed an oval ring measuring nearly 200 metres across its long axis and more than 150 metres across its short axis. Two concentric containing walls constructed of brick-faced concrete were built, about 3 metres thick, 6.5 metres high and about 50 metres apart. The space between the walls was then filled with concrete to just above the level of the bed of the lake.

At this point the whole foundation was divided into four sectors to leave a gap, about 5 metres wide, corresponding with the long and short axes. Four tunnels with travertine walls and concrete vaults were built into these gaps with main drainage conduits a little over 1 metre wide running beneath them. These drains sloped outwards at an incline of 1:40. When they were excavated during the 1970s some of the wooden shuttering used to contain the concrete was found still in situ.

When the oval area with the foundations was cleared the foundations of several earlier buildings that had been destroyed in the fire of AD 64 were left in place, as was normal Roman practice – early in the second century Trajan was to build the first of Rome's great bathing complexes

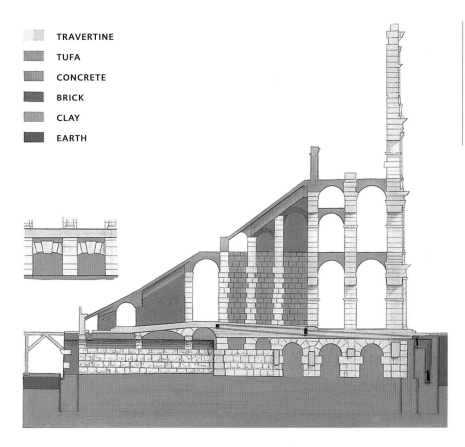

TRAVERTINE

TUFA

CONCRETE

BRICK

CLAY

EARTH

A diagrammatic section of the north-eastern end of the Colosseum showing the foundations and the superstructure. *Inset* The travertine substructures beneath the façade.

on top of Nero's Golden House and he never bothered to demolish it completely. With the ground completely levelled, the builders laid a 40-centimetre thick layer of concrete over the bed of the lake, with a gap about 0.5 metres wide around the perimeter for drainage. The concrete floor was probably laid at this time to stop the water from seeping in and turning the site into a quagmire.

Everything was now prepared for the second phase of construction. The foundations still had to be built up for a further 6.5 metres but before that was done the substructure under the seating areas was installed. The concrete surface was smoothed off with a fine lime mortar made from powdered travertine to bed the lowest course of supports for the super-structure that would be built in blocks of hard travertine. The travertine substructure within the foundations mirrored the superstructure but was more massive. The whole seating area was designed to rest on a series of concentric arcades built of travertine. There were 80 arches in the outer arcade that formed the façade of the Amphitheatre. Ultimately the lowest

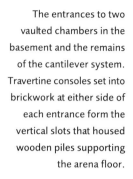

The entrances to two vaulted chambers in the basement and the remains of the cantilever system. Travertine consoles set into brickwork at either side of each entrance form the vertical slots that housed wooden piles supporting the arena floor.

level would be embedded in concrete but work could begin on the ground and first floor before the foundations were complete.

Both inside and outside the *cavea* there was a containing wall for the upper foundations constructed in brick-faced concrete. The inside containing wall would also form the perimeter wall of the basement below the arena. A complex of walls was later built to support the wooden flooring of the arena but in the early days of the Amphitheatre the perimeter wall had to accommodate lifts to raise animals and props up into the arena and also provide a cantilever system to support the wooden floor of the arena. The four axial tunnels could be used for bringing in animals and props secretly from outside but lifts were needed to bring them up into the arena. To allow these functions the brick perimeter wall was indented with 36 shallow vaulted chambers. These were only just over 1.5 metres deep but they were 3 metres wide and over 5 metres high. The vaults at the top were faced with slim upright bricks laid on a wooden former or centre then cemented together. The animal lifts operated within these chambers, raised by a mechanism set into a wedge-shaped hole at the vault. The upper part was probably barred in with a grille fitted with a gate to let the animals out onto a ramp and then through a trap door leading up into the arena. Confronted by the screaming mob, the animals would not have entered the arena willingly but would have been goaded with spears or flaming torches. Only a short time after the Amphitheatre was opened a mezzanine floor was fitted into the lift shafts with a hole in the middle to let the lifts through. This allowed a couple of men to stand on either side of the lift, prodding the terrified animals through the bars.

The arena floor was supported by a system of cantilevers, which were set into the brickwork between the vaulted chambers. This consisted of a long 44-centimetre wide vertical slot in the brickwork to house a wooden beam, with a travertine console set into the brickwork on either side. Travertine blocks with slots of similar dimensions in them were set into the floor of the basement at intervals of 6 or 7 metres. Several of these have been found still in situ. These travertine blocks housed the 6-metre high wooden piles supporting the arena. The huge 6–7-metre span, at least in the area next to the perimeter wall, was braced in the centre by trusses resting on the two consoles. (The vaulted chambers and the cantilever system are described in further detail in Appendix I.)

The four putative lift shafts at the ends on either side of the two long axis tunnels were not bricked in across the back but formed entrances to four underground galleries some 20 metres long. Work was already quite well advanced and the brickwork several courses high when the architects realized that they had made no allowance for housing the boats to be used in sea-battles, nor for the machinery necessary for raising large scenery and props. There are telltale traces of demolished walls on the floor of the basement that would appear to support this hypothesis. Modifications during work in progress were a common feature of Roman construction – the width of Hadrian's Wall was changed after work had started and there is evidence of constant revisions in Caesar's siege works at Alesia in France.

The modifications at the Colosseum must have been carried out immediately as the work involved inserting travertine arches into the vaulted ceiling. These can be clearly seen dividing up the shuttered concrete vaulting of the galleries. The short axis tunnels also display this feature. Since these subterranean arches radiated out from set points on the long axis, the new galleries fanned out on either side of the two tunnels, allowing small rooms and spiral staircases to be inserted into the wedge shape that this design created. The tunnels and galleries were walled with large, squared, travertine blocks, their vaulted ceilings shuttered and the concrete laid. The stonemasons smoothed off the blocks in the axis tunnels but left most of the travertine blocks in the side galleries in a rougher state – only one wall, at the west end, was properly finished off. The brickwork along the

The interior of the Colosseum viewed from the eastern end. The underground corridors beneath the arena floor are labelled A–H here, following the naming convention adopted by most historians and achaeologists, with the two corridors A at the perimeter and corridor H running down the middle. They are referred to by these letters in the text.

The first annular corridor
on the north side of the
Colosseum.

south side of the basement was coated with *opus signinum*, a type of coarse waterproof mortar traditionally used to line aqueducts, cisterns and swimming pools. However, there is no trace of the north side of the basement being lined in this way.

THE SEATING SYSTEM

Work started on the *cavea* as soon as the foundations had been built up to basement level. The lowest level of the travertine arch system rested on these lower foundations and rose 6.5 metres above the basement to what would ultimately be the ground level of the building. Once the containing walls also reached this level they were filled with layered concrete and topped with three layers of travertine slabs to produce the ground floor of the building. The travertine arcades were continued upwards, the individual stone blocks being held together with iron clamps. The arcades rose in tiers like a modern reinforced concrete building, allowing the builders to work on more than one level at the same time. The inside circuit, which supported the ringside seating reserved for the senators, was only 5 metres above ground level but the outer circuits rose to a final height of 48.5 metres. Ultimately, the level of the whole surrounding area was raised another 2 metres and the piazza surrounding the building was paved with travertine blocks.

The seven circuits of upright travertine structures that had been installed in the foundations were also built upwards to form flush vertical piers within the thickness of the wall, being converted into arches when required. The walls were joined together with concrete barrel vaults to form wedge-shaped radial passages, aligned with the arches, into which the stairways were fitted. The passageways radiated from points on the main axis in order to form an oval. The radiating walls and arches that formed these passages conformed to a standard pattern that could be modified as required. At the ground-floor level the spaces between the travertine ribs were filled in with tufa blocks to form walls that were occasionally pierced by an arched doorway. On the first floor the spaces between the ribs were filled with brick-faced concrete. An allowance for an arched doorway was made in each section – the bricks forming the arches are still there – though in some cases these gaps were filled in.

The 7-metre high arches of the three outer arcades were joined laterally by concrete barrel vaults to form two outer corridors running round the building in a complete circuit. The innermost circuits of travertine uprights were joined in the same way to form an internal circuit. There was one further ring corridor close to the arena, constructed of brick-faced concrete faced with marble. It was especially grand because this was the passageway that led to the ringside seats where the VIPs sat. This type of design of arcades and vaulted radial passages was not new – it had been employed in the construction of the Theatre of Pompey over a hundred years before.

The first floor of the Amphitheatre was supported by the outer two corridors and the vaults above the travertine and tufa walls. The outermost corridor was very similar, though less massive, than the one below it. The inner corridor, however, was reduced in height to insert a mezzanine above it. This may have been the level the builders had reached by the time Vespasian dedicated the building in AD 79, shortly before his death. By the time the Colosseum was officially inaugurated by Vespasian's son Titus a

This bronze sesterce, minted during the eighth consulship of Titus (before 1 July, AD 80), is the earliest representation of the Colosseum. The coin also shows the Meta Sudans fountain on the left and a two-level portico on the right. The statue of a four-horse chariot is framed in the central arch of the second level with more statues in the arches either side of it and on the third level. Large shields alternate with windows around the attic wall, and the awning beams are visible above. The *cavea* is shown with tiered seating areas, stairs, balconies and the emperor's box in the centre.

Opposite
The architectural orders
with (from bottom to top)
their Doric, Ionic and
Corinthian columns.

year later, it is likely that a further floor had been added. There is some evidence to suggest that the façade was only three storeys high at this stage and this is how the building appears in a relief on the Tomb of the Haterii (reproduced on page 60), which has been dated to the reign of Titus's brother Domitian (AD 81-96). A coin minted a few years earlier, during Titus's reign, shows the complete building, including a fourth storey. This is by no means proof of what the Colosseum really looked like at the time but can only be viewed as a projection of its intended design.

The outer arcade forming the façade of the Colosseum ultimately rose to a height of nearly 50 metres. On each level the arches were framed with engaged columns, half columns carved into the travertine blocks surmounted with an architrave and cornice, creating the effect of a combined colonnade and arcade. This architectural device was very popular, having been used previously on the buildings around the Forum Romanum and on the Theatre of Marcellus. The bottom storey had columns of the Doric order, the second of the Ionic order and the third of the Corinthian order. The fourth storey consisted of a plain wall with Corinthian pilasters, flat half columns creating a similar effect to the lower levels.

The radial passages housed stairways leading up to the various seating zones, with a final flight emerging into the *cavea*. These entrances were called *vomitoria* and because they created a bit of a bottleneck people were often in danger of being crushed, both on their way in and on their way out. In certain places there was a drop of as much as 3 metres into the stairwell from the seating area above and though there were stone balustrades to help stop people falling, such accidents were not always prevented.

Several decorated fragments of the stairwell balustrades have been found at the Colosseum. The balustrade above the portal appears always to have been decorated with spirals of acanthus leaves, flowers and palmettes. Similar balustrade slabs have been found in the amphitheatre at Capua in Campania. Only the side facing the arena is decorated. The categories of spectators allowed in that particular area appear to have been inscribed on the plain side of the balustrade facing the spectators. The balustrades flanking the entrance have various decorations. Two of the six fragments found at the Colosseum show dogs hunting deer, the rest depicting other creatures, such as dolphins, griffins and sphinxes.

At the time of the opening the corridors and stairways were plastered and painted in bright colours – red, green, yellow and black. Although none

of this survives in situ, fragments of painted plaster have been discovered. After the disastrous fire of AD 217 these areas were redecorated with a more sombre red and white plaster and much of this was still in place when the Colosseum was first excavated by archaeologists at the end of the eighteenth century.

The seating capacity of the Colosseum has long been debated. The problem of obtaining an accurate estimate stems from the fact that amphitheatres of this type did not provide individual seats as such but had tiers or terraces of broad stone steps designed to accommodate a certain number of people. The Roman architect Vitruvius (*fl.* first century BC) recommended that seating steps should be 60–65 centimetres deep and no more than 40 centimetres high. The width of each individual seating space depended on where it was: the higher up the building you went the less room you got. The amount of space allocated per person somewhere in the middle of the *cavea* is thought to have been about 45 centimetres.

The common people were expected to bring their own cushions to sit on (a convention that continues to this day in certain open-air concert and opera venues in Italy, such as the amphitheatre in Verona) but spectators of high rank on the podium would have been provided with chairs. No traces of the imperial box or the magistrates' box remain.

The seating in the Colosseum broadly reflected the Roman class system and was divided into five levels. Roughly speaking these were equivalent to the divisions of a modern auditorium: the ringside seats or podium were at the very front, followed by the front stalls, the back or rear stalls, the circle or dress circle and, right at the top, the upper circle (or balcony, gallery or gods). The word *maenianum*, which was used to describe the levels in an amphitheatre, comes from Maenius, a fourth-century Roman magistrate and one-time official censor. In 348 BC he devised a system of seating on wooden balconies above the shops in the marketplace so that people had a good view of the shows taking place down below.

Fragments of the balustrades surrounding the *vomitoria* have been found (*inset*), enabling a reconstruction of a *vomitorium* to be made.

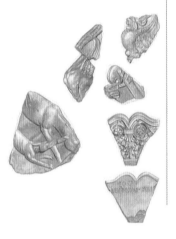

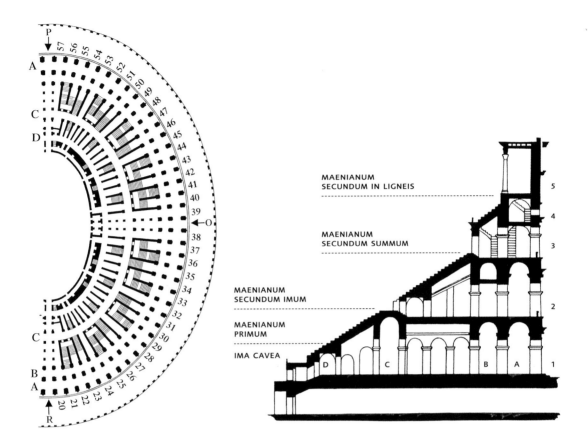

The first section of seating (*ima cavea*), commonly known as the podium, afforded the best view of the arena and was reserved for the VIPs. The podium in the Colosseum consisted of four broad, white marble steps or terraces, and the senators and their guests would sit on chairs placed there specially for each show. This area was separated from the arena by a marble balustrade, which was a necessary barrier between the action and the audience, especially when the wild animals came on. The spectators in this section enjoyed the luxury of their own cloakroom and latrines, and surviving inscriptions indicate that some of them had regular family places.

The second level (*maenianum primum*) had a much bigger capacity than the first – eight or nine marble terraces – and this area was allocated to members of the equestrian class. Above this, the third level (*maenianum secundum imum*) consisted of 19 or 20 terraces and held even more spectators than the second. The ordinary citizens sat here and on the fourth level (*maenianum secundum summum*), which was divided into numbered sections known as wedges (*cunei*). It is not known exactly how many terraces there

Plan and section diagram of the seating area.

A First annular corridor
B Second annular corridor
C Third annular corridor
D Fourth annular corridor
O Magistrates' entrance
P Porta Triumphalis (ceremonial entrance of the gladiators)
R Porta Libitinensis (the 'Death Gate')

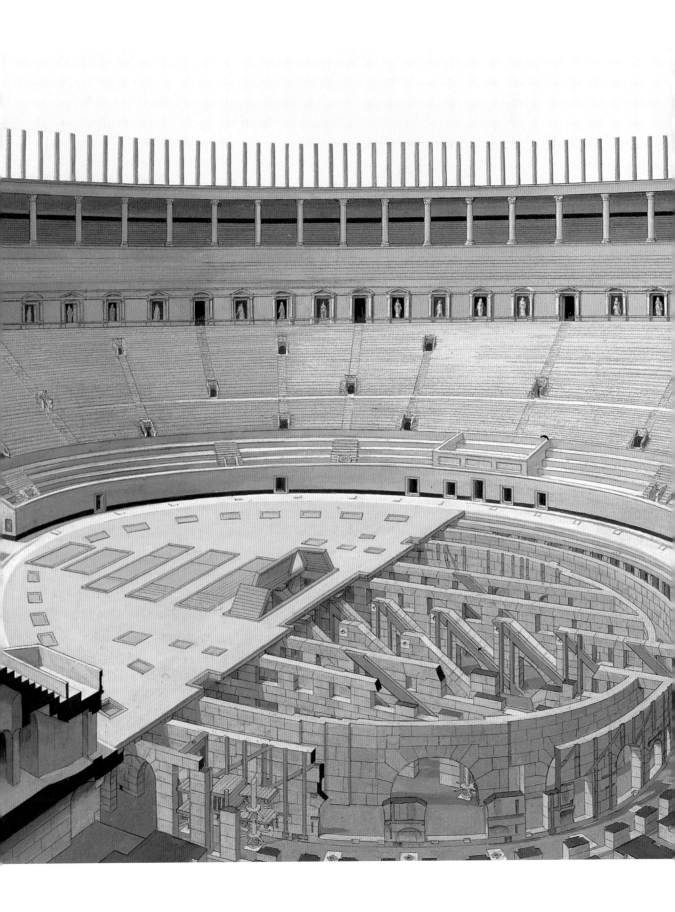

Previous pages
A cut-away section of the
Colosseum at the time of
Domitian showing the
various corridors and
vomitoria. The trapdoors
in the arena correspond to
the position of the lifts and
ramps in the basement.

were at this level but it is estimated that there were probably ten or eleven. The terraces in the third and fourth sections were made of white travertine. The section right at the top of the Amphitheatre (*maenianum secundum in ligneis*), sometimes known as the attic, is where the lowest class of people sat, on wooden terraces. This tier, with an estimated ten or eleven terraces like level four, was divided into 80 wedges corresponding to the arches of the arcade at ground level. As well as being cheaper and easier, wood was used for this level because of the need to reduce the outward thrust on the external wall. This was not a problem at the lower levels as the concrete vaults on which the seating rested sloped inwards, creating a system of buttressing.

Each tier of seating was designed to rise at a carefully calculated angle to give the spectators the best view possible of the arena. The second tier inclines at an angle of 30 degrees and the third tier is set at 35 degrees. It is impossible to measure the angle of incline above this, unfortunately, because not enough of the building has survived to yield an accurate estimate.

It was Rome's first emperor, Augustus, who first lifted the ban on stone amphitheatres and it was he who formalized the social divisions that are reflected in the Colosseum's seating arrangements. This was all part of the liberal reform and social legislation that he instigated. One of his innovations was to introduce a system of numbered seats at the *munera*: everyone going to an amphitheatre was given a token (*tessera*) telling them which seat had been reserved for them. This was a subtle form of social control for it meant that the sponsors and organizers of the games could determine exactly where everyone sat. As most of the shows were free, the spectators had little choice but to accept their allotted places.

Augustus was also responsible for segregating certain sections of society in the amphitheatres and there is evidence that the Colosseum followed his scheme, with specially designated seating areas for visiting ambassadors and diplomats, soldiers, married men, adolescent noblemen and their tutors, women, poor commoners, foreigners and slaves. A few inscriptions indicating which sector was reserved for which group can still be seen on surviving tiers in the Colosseum, such as *Loca Bentiorum* (the places of the Bentii) engraved on a balustrade slab. Augustus kept the men away from the women and military personnel away from the civilians. He allowed the Vestal Virgins (priestesses of the temple) the privilege of sitting on the podium facing the praetor's box but banished all other women to the

All the original seating in the Colosseum has been destroyed. This section of seating for the equestrian class was reconstructed in the 1930s over the fourth annular corridor – the marble-lined senatorial corridor with its cloak-rooms and latrines.

fourth level. Sometimes he banned women altogether from certain contests.

The Roman priesthood, like society in general, was strictly hierarchical, with those at the top drawn from the patrician class, and so the clerics would be dispersed throughout the different sections of an amphitheatre according to their status. A marble tablet that was found on the Via Campana just outside Rome confirms this practice and, furthermore, gives us an indication of how sophisticated the seating system was in the Colosseum. (The man in charge of deciding who sat where when it was first built was Laberius Maximus, who was also responsible for doling out free grain to the poor at the time.) The inscription on the tablet is a record of the places allocated to the members of the religious order known as the Brotherhood of the Arvales (*Fratres Arvales*) for the inaugural ceremony in

An artist's impression of the decorated interior of the magistrates' ceremonial entrance on the north side of the Colosseum (*right*) and a photograph of the entrance arch today.

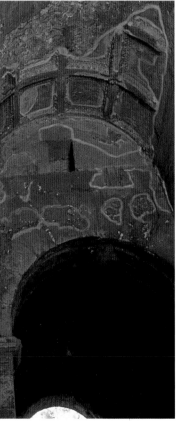

AD 80. It shows that they were assigned places on the second, third and fourth levels and specifies in Roman feet the amount of space they were entitled to occupy. Not included in this list are the 12 members of the brotherhood who were also senators. They would automatically have been entitled to ringside seats on the podium.

Scholars have puzzled over this data for years because it appears to offer the key to an important question: how many people could you get into the Colosseum in AD 80? In 1925 the German archaeologist A. Von Gerkan published his answer: 45,000 people seated, with extra standing room on the top level. According to the calendar of AD 354 the capacity was 87,000 places (*loca*), but this is generally thought to mean Roman feet. The controversy appears to centre on the definition of the Latin word *locus* – did it mean 'place' or 'seat' or was it another term for the measurement known as a Roman foot (approximately 30 centimetres)? The matter has never been resolved completely to everyone's satisfaction but most people now settle for an estimate of around 50,000.

Entrance number LIII (53). The numbers above 32 of the 80 entrance arches are still visible.

MAKING AN ENTRANCE

There were 80 entrances altogether in the outer arcade of the Colosseum at ground level and 76 of them, which were used by the general public, were identified by a number inscribed in the stone above the archway. The Roman numerals on just over a third of these entrances, numbers XXIII–LIV (23–54), can still be seen today. The remaining entrances, one at each end of the long and short axes, were not numbered as they each had a specific function.

The entrance on the south side, on the short axis, was reserved exclusively for the emperor and his entourage. This was destroyed in the Middle Ages and only the inner portion survives, and that bears no trace of its original decoration. The emperor's private box, which must have been here, supported on the two inner travertine arcades, has also disappeared.

Detail from a bas-relief from the Tomb of the Haterii in Rome. The Colosseum is shown with statues in the arches of the first and second levels and a triumphal arch surmounted by a four-horse chariot in front of the imperial entrance.

The only visual reference to the imperial entrance that survives today is the relief on the Tomb of the Haterii. This shows a gateway with a triumphal arch above it and the representation of a four-horse chariot (*quadriga*), a vehicle usually associated with figures of authority. Also depicted are three huge eagles and the statues of three gods – Hercules, Apollo and Aesculapius – below them. It is generally accepted that the creator of this relief was a bit free in his interpretations and so it should not be seen as a totally reliable source.

The basic design of the Colosseum is symmetrical so it is reasonable to assume that the magistrates' entrance, at the opposite end of the short axis, on the north side, will give a pretty good idea of what the emperor's entrance was like for this, fortunately, has survived almost intact. It is in fact a triple entrance, being a main archway with a matching pair of smaller ones on either side. There are still fragments of stucco decoration on the upper walls and vaulting to be seen in the area beyond the two outer corridors of the magistrates' entrance. An etching by the Dutch artist M. D'Overbeke published in 1763 shows us what this stucco work looked like, together with the walls below, which were faced with white marble. Outside, the balustrade above the magistrates' entrance is broken away, suggesting that there may have been a pediment here.

The entrances at either end of the long axis are also triple archways and they were used exclusively by the performers. The entrance at the west end, the Porta Triumphalis, was where the gladiatorial procession (*pompa*) entered and the entrance at the east end, the Porta Libitinensis, the so-called Gate of Death, was where the gladiators exited, many of them, as the name suggests, as corpses. The area underneath this entrance gave access to two spiral staircases, which allowed the gladiators, animal fighters and handlers, referees, stretcher-bearers and others involved in the games to pass unseen through a tunnel leading to the Ludus Magnus, the gladiator school next door.

The compartments formed by the rising network of vaults and passages housed a system of radiating staircases, ramps and ring corridors with plastered and painted walls. The innermost ring corridor, which was lined with marble, was reserved for senators and gave them access to their seating on the podium alongside the arena. The outer two ring corridors at the first two levels form an open arcade, but at the first level the individual arches were fitted with iron gates and these could be closed to stop people getting in when the Amphitheatre was not in use. The gates could also be used to control the crowds entering the building, channelling them towards the system of stairways and passages which led directly to their reserved seats. These and the inner ring corridors provided separate access to each wedge of seating and to each level within that area.

To get an idea of the complexity of the access system we can look at one representative quarter – that stretching from the entrance to the right of the magistrates, entrance numbered XXXVIIII (39) as far round as the entrance next to the western ceremonial entrance LVII (57). All except four of these retain their Roman numerals above the arch. The senators reached their seats on the podium via the passages on either side of the main entrances at the ends of the long and short axes. These led directly to the fourth or innermost ring corridor. Those with seats in the lowest public area used passages XLV (45) or XLIX (49), which brought them to the third ring corridor. They then took one of the four flights of stairs up to their seats. Those with seats on the levels above this had first to reach the second level, which was accessed indirectly by any of the stairs leading off the second ring corridor, or directly by any of the stairs leading off the outer side of the third ring corridor. From here they would either have taken a stairway to the upper seats or passed through one of the passages leading to the lower seating of their area.

The higher levels could only be reached from the outer ring corridors on the second floor. From here, stairways built against the inside of the second

The magistrates' entrance on the north side. Although the balustrade above the main arch is long gone, a pediment is thought to have projected out from it, supporting a statue of a four-horse chariot.

The cornice around the top of the external wall of the attic on the northeast side. Wooden masts placed through these square apertures and held by the travertine brackets beneath them supported the awning (*velarium*).

arcade led up to a mezzanine, obviously inserted as an afterthought when the seating was installed at the upper levels. The stairways built against the opposite side of the same arcade led up to a low outer ring corridor inserted immediately below the original vault of the second floor corridor. This mini ring corridor received light only from small apertures in the outer façade. This is a later modification, almost certainly from the reign of Domitian. Stairways grafted onto the outer wall of this led to the topmost level, the balcony with its wooden seating, clearly also an afterthought. Most of this area was severely damaged in the fire of AD 217 and had to be rebuilt.

The attic seating was covered by a portico running all round the top of the *cavea*. This kind of arrangement is known in other amphitheatres of the Roman world but usually it just forms a covered walkway at the top of the building. A number of marble fragments surviving from the portico allow it to be reconstructed. The columns were made in a single piece, of either grey granite or cipolin, a type of green-veined marble from Euboea off the eastern coast of Greece. The bases and capitals were of white marble and the capitals were carved in the Corinthian and composite orders.

THE AWNING

Like many other comparable public buildings, the Colosseum was fitted with a huge canvas awning (*velarium*) that protected the spectators from the sun. A wall painting from Pompeii drawn to record a riot between rival supporters in AD 59 shows the amphitheatre there with an awning draped on poles over part of the seating. Awnings were clearly a very attractive amenity; there are graffiti from Pompeii advertising gladiatorial games, that include the words *vela erunt*: 'there will be awnings'.

The awning in Rome was much more sophisticated than the one in Pompeii. There are 240 projecting brackets around the topmost part of the Colosseum and masts inserted through square holes in the cornice rested on these brackets. The rigging that supported the awning was attached to these masts. Detachments of sailors from the Roman fleets at Misenum and Ravenna were billeted in Rome in order to maintain and operate the rigging, and it has been estimated that at least 1000 men would have been required to lower and raise the awning as required; they would have been working from within the wooden roof above the attic. On the inside of the eastern

A wall painting from Pompeii showing the riot in the amphitheatre there in AD 59 which resulted in the venue being closed on Nero's orders for ten years. The painting is also unique in depicting an amphitheatre with its awning extended.

The awning (*velarium*) was hauled into position by sailors. Traces of a double flight of steps they used to reach the top of the colonnade are clearly visible.

end of the uppermost level of the outer wall, above entrances 26 and 27, one can see the remains of the double flight of steps that the sailors would have used to reach the roof of the portico. There was a matching set of steps at the other end of the *cavea* above entrances 50 and 51. These are obviously later insertions as they are built across windows. We can assume that similar flights existed above entrances 12 and 13 and also above entrances 64 and 65.

There is no agreement among scholars about how exactly the Colosseum awning worked. Most envisage 240 ropes extending from the masts on top of the outer wall to an oval rope in the centre, which formed an opening (*oculus*) through which the sun shone on the arena. The awning itself was somehow stretched out over the 240 ropes. Such a system would have been practical but would have required considerable teamwork from those who operated it. Attempts to recreate this system for a television programme a few years ago failed because it was only tried in one sector of the Amphitheatre. The secret is that the system can only work if the web of ropes is winched up from all 240 points at the same time and at the same rate. This could explain why disciplined sailors from the fleet were employed. A recent estimate by a professional tent and awning manufacturer suggests that the ropes and light linen required to cover the Colosseum in this manner would weigh about 24.3 tonnes. Others have suggested that masts were used in a system similar to that which appears to be in use in the amphitheatre riot painting from Pompeii. This is likely to have been the case anyway when the Colosseum was inaugurated in AD 80 because the fourth level of the building had probably not yet been added. The celebrations took place over a period of three months during the summer so some form of shade for the spectators would have been vital.

There was a travertine pavement outside the Colosseum, 17.5 metres wide, with a row of 80 stone posts along its outer edge. The five posts that remain lean inwards towards the Amphitheatre and each has four pairs of square holes cut into the inner face. It is tempting to assume that these bollards were meant to anchor the winches used to raise the awning. However, they are simply embedded in the earth rather than built with proper foundations and so would not have withstood the strain. They are leaning inwards because earth has been sliding down the hillside for centuries and the weight of the soil has pushed them over. They are thought to be all that remains of a barrier that was originally fitted with iron railings, and possibly with gates as well. Similar stone posts have been found outside the amphitheatre at Ancient Capua (Santa Maria Capua Vetere), where it is believed they formed part of a crowd control barrier.

These five remaining stone posts are thought to have formed part of a crowd control barrier. Originally, 80 would have been set into the travertine pavement, encircling the building.

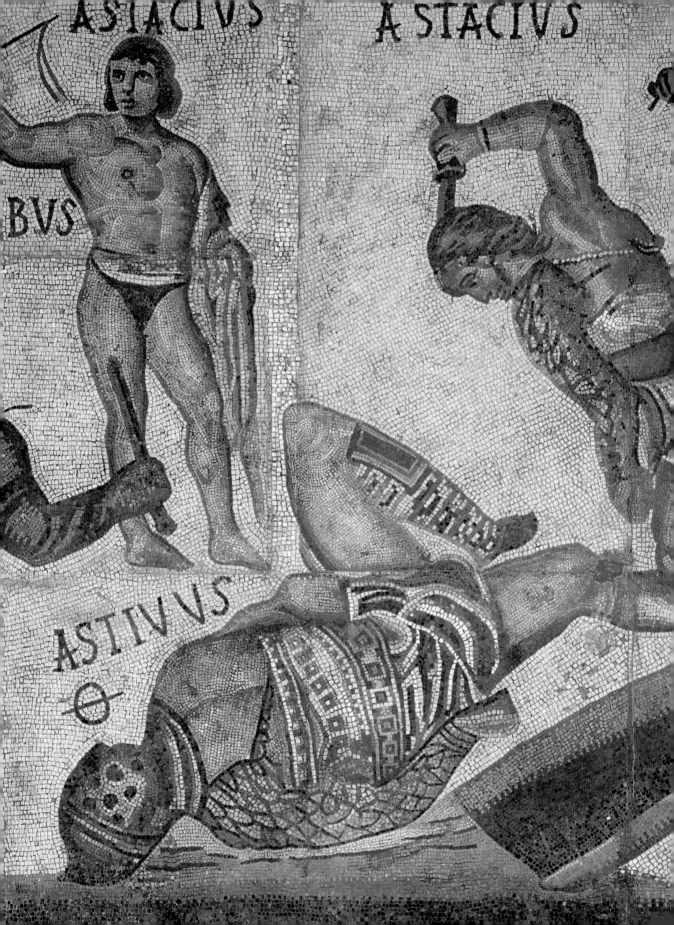

ENTER THE GLADIATORS

The earliest gladiators were drawn from the various tribes conquered by the Romans, and their names – the Samnites, the Thracians, the Gauls – reflected this. Different types of gladiators were also distinguished by their weapons and armour. The *equites* fought each other on horseback. The heavily armoured *hoplomachus* was often matched against the *murmillo* – the fish man – with his large rectangular shield. The well-protected *secutor*, who carried a shield, a sword and wore a distinctive helmet, often pursued the *retiarius*, whose only defences were a trident and a net.

Opposite
This fourth-century AD mosaic, one of five found in Torre Nova on the Via Casilina and now housed in the Villa Borghese in Rome, shows gladiators in combat. In this scene a *retiarius* is about to kill a fallen *secutor*.

Most of the men who became gladiators in Rome were enslaved prisoners of war. The Romans considered all people who opposed them to be no better than criminals deserving death, and this is reflected in the Latin word for slave, *servus*, which means 'one who is saved'. This belief is expressed in the *Res Gestae*, a paean to Augustus's achievements: 'The nations that could be safely pardoned I chose to save rather than to eradicate.' The same attitude survives into the Christian era. Constantine the Great, for instance, said of the German tribe, the Bructeri, that they were a people whose 'barbarism and treachery made them useless as slaves'. Since he believed they would serve no purpose to Roman society he had all of the prisoners of war executed in the arena.

THE ORIGINS OF GLADIATORIAL COMBAT

Scholars have been trying to identify the true origins of gladiatorial combat for centuries. The ancient regions of Etruria, Campania and Lucania have all been suggested as the likely birthplace and there are tomb paintings from the fourth century BC in central and southern Italy that show armed men duelling. Some of these paintings also depict chariot races and men fighting bare-knuckle, which are activities that the Romans also went in for. It is likely that duelling displays originally formed part of the ritual of human sacrifice, a funerary practice that goes back as far as the Bronze Age in Europe. It is certainly known from Roman writers such as Servius, Livy, Ausonius and Tertullian that people in pre-Christian Rome discharged their duty to the dead, or at least to the souls or spirits of the dead (*manes*), by offering another death. The fresco from the François Tomb at Vulci showing Achilles killing Trojan prisoners in the presence of Charun, the Etruscan god of the underworld, supports this belief.

The Christian theologian Tertullian (AD *c*. 160–*c*. 240) offers an explanation for why a practice that was originally a solemn funeral rite gradually became part of the celebrations at a wake, a bit of entertainment to accompany the feasting:

> The ancients thought that by this sort of spectacle they rendered service
> to the dead, after they had tempered it with a more cultured form of
> cruelty. For of old, in the belief that the souls of the dead are propitiated

with human blood, they used at funerals to sacrifice captives or slaves of poor quality. Afterwards it seemed good to obscure their impiety by making it a pleasure. So after the persons procured had been trained in such arms as they then had and as best they might – their training was to learn to be killed! – they then did them to death on the appointed funeral day at the tombs. So they found comfort for death in murder …

The Romans chose slaves or prisoners of war to be sacrificed because they were foreigners, non-citizens, and people who had no social status were always expendable.

The Roman writer Valerius Maximus (*c.* 20 BC–AD *c.* 50) provides the earliest known record of a gladiatorial-style fight in Rome itself, and it formed part of the funeral ceremony held for a consul called Brutus Pera in 264 BC. Several tribes allied to Rome sent captives to be sacrificed on his behalf but two of his sons, Marcus and Decimus, selected six of the men,

This fresco from the François tomb at Vulci shows Achilles cutting the throat of a Trojan prisoner. Charun, with his hammer, is standing behind and Ajax in a white tunic to the right of him.

This tomb painting from Paestum in southern Italy dates from the fourth century BC and shows gladiators long before they appeared in Rome.

paired them off and ordered them to fight to the death in front of the mourners. This event took place in a cattle market down by the River Tiber, the Forum Boarium. It clearly sparked off a fashion and soon it became the custom for aristocratic families to offer some sort of staged combat at a funeral.

As these events became more popular so they grew in size and scale. It is recorded that 22 pairs of combatants fought to the death at the funeral of one Marcus Aemilius Lepidus in 216 BC; 33 years later, at the funeral of a man called Publius Licinius, the record had increased to 60 pairs. It was said that during one performance of *The Mother-in-Law*, a play by Terence (*c.* 190-159 BC), the entire audience left halfway through when word went round that there was a fight due to start elsewhere – probably at the funeral in 167 BC of Lucius Aemilius Paullus, the conqueror of Macedonia.

The *munera* were evidently a form of conspicuous consumption – the number of gladiators your family could rustle up when you died was a public statement of your wealth and position in society. The favoured venue for such spectacles switched from the Forum Boarium to the Forum Romanum, between the Capitoline and the Palatine Hill.

THE HENLEY COLLEGE LIBRARY

GLADIATORS OF THE ROMAN REPUBLIC

The word 'gladiator' comes from the Latin *gladius*, meaning 'sword'. (The gladiolus plant gets its name from the same source, in reference to its stiff, sword-shaped leaves.) This would indicate that a gladiator was originally a swordsman. The term first appears in the works of Cato (234-149 BC) and Lucilius (*c.* 180-102 BC). It is significant that the Roman legionaries were the only soldiers who carried a sword as a primary weapon, and this fact has led to speculation that it was they who first trained the gladiators before allowing them to fight in public.

The earliest Roman gladiators belonged to distinct tribes and their names reflect this – the Samnites, the Thracians and the Gauls, for example. These were the people who had been conquered by the Romans. Later gladiators were allocated to these national groups by their trainers.

THE SAMNITES

The first type of gladiator to crop up in the published sources is the Samnite, who is generally considered to be the prototype for all the Roman gladiators. No one knows whether the original Samnite gladiators were volunteers or whether they were prisoners of war. Livy describes what the Samnite soldiers looked like during the battle against the Samnites fought in Campania in 310 BC:

> The Samnites, besides their other warlike preparations, had made their
> battle line to glitter with new and splendid arms. There were two corps: the
> shields of the one were inlaid with gold and of the other with silver. The
> shape of the shield was this: the upper part, where it protected the breast
> and shoulders, was rather broad with a level top; below it was somewhat
> tapering, to make it easier to handle. They wore a sponge (*spongia*) to
> protect the breast and the left leg was covered with a greave. Their helmets
> were crested, to make their stature appear greater. The tunics of the gilded
> warriors were multicoloured; those of the silver ones were dazzling white
> linen. The latter had silver sheaths and baldrics: the former gilded sheaths
> and baldrics, and their horses had gold embroidered saddlecloths.

Livy goes on to record that Rome's allies at the time, the Campanians, 'in consequence of their pride and in hatred of the Samnites, equipped after

A bas-relief from Amiternum near Aquila in Italy dating from the middle of the first century BC probably showing two Samnite gladiators.

this fashion the gladiators who furnished them entertainment at their feasts and bestowed on them the name of Samnites'. If this account is authentic then it supports Livy's claim that gladiatorial contests were taking place in southern Italy at least half a century before the events at Brutus Pera's funeral in Rome.

The shield that Livy describes appears to be a variant of the Roman legionary shield (*scutum*). These do occasionally appear in contemporary paintings but it is usually clear that they are captured spoils. His use of the word *spongia* to describe the breastplate may be a copyist's error or it may mean 'mail', which could be said to have a sponge-like appearance. If it *was* mail then Livy may indeed have been recording the introduction of a new type of armour. (There is evidence that mail was beginning to appear in Celtic burials at about this time.)

Though it has proved impossible to link the dozens of tomb paintings in Campania and Lucania that show armed men fighting duels with later representations of Roman gladiators, scholars have noted various similarities. The southern duellists are all depicted with helmets and most of them are wearing greaves (leg-protectors) too, and though they are seldom shown in body armour they are often seen wearing the broad Samnite bronze belt. However, their weapons of choice were either spears or javelins and sometimes a round Greek shield, whereas the gladiators of the Roman

Republic normally fought with a short sword, with the sword-arm protected by a segmented arm-guard (*manica*), and various types of shield.

From Livy's description we would expect a Samnite warrior of the second century BC to be armed with mail, a single greave, an Italic spindle-boss shield and a spear or javelin. A bas-relief sculpture from Aquila in central Italy dating from the first century BC probably shows two Samnite gladiators, each wearing a mail shirt and a single greave on the left leg, and armed with a spear and a long, rectangular, spindle-boss shield. A squire stands behind each warrior holding three spare weapons.

After the Romans finally defeated the Samnites and other dissident Italian tribes in 90 BC all Italians were granted Roman citizenship and the gladiators known by that name begin to disappear from the lists.

THE *PAEGNIARII*

The *paegniarii* were a type of comic gladiator who entertained the public in the warm-up before the real gladiators appeared. They would often perform again during the intervals between contests. They were in fact actors masquerading as gladiators and like the Samnites, whose style of combat they parodied, most of them came from Campania. There is some evidence for their existence there from the fourth century BC though the practice of staging mock duels did not reach Rome for another two hundred years. Lucilius saw one of these fights at Capua in 119 BC and considered it worth recording. Performing a show that came from a traditional south Italian repertoire of farces, the 'loser' of the pair had a grotesque appearance with a huge tooth sticking out of his mouth (probably a mask) and both wore helmets with feathers in them. At the end of the fight the 'victor' took the feathers from the 'loser' and added them to the five feathers already in his own helmet. There is abundant archaeological evidence for helmets with two feather holders but the 'Warriors Return' tomb painting at Capua shows a warrior with five feathers.

Paegniarii (mock fighters) shown on a third-century AD mosaic from the villa of Nennig, Germany.

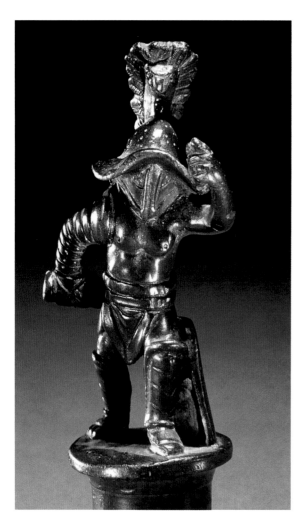

A finial in the form of a Thracian wearing a crested helmet, greaves and an arm-guard. A small rectangular shield rests at his side.

THE GAULS

The Gaul was probably a very early gladiator type. They increased in popularity following Caesar's conquest of Gaul in the first century BC, after which time thousands of captives were despatched to Rome. These gladiators were originally armed with the same type of weapons that a typical Gallic warrior would have carried: a spear or a straight-bladed cut-and-thrust sword, about 60 centimetres long, and a long, flat shield with a spindle boss. It is likely that they subsequently adopted the long slashing sword that became the weapon of choice among the Gallic military later on. By the first century BC they had started wearing protective headgear (Gallic soldiers usually went into battle bareheaded) and this is when the Gauls came to be known as *murmillones* – a term derived from the name of a Greek fish (*murmuros*), which was the emblem that appeared on their helmets.

THE THRACIANS

The Thracians (who occupied the territory that is roughly equivalent to modern Bulgaria) were a warlike people who constantly clashed with the Romans. As a result many Thracians were captured as prisoners of war and became gladiators, with a reputation as fearsome fighters. They retained two pieces of native military equipment: a helmet with a crest that curved forward and a curved sword (*sica*). They also carried a small, rectangular, semi-cylindrical shield and wore thigh-length greaves and a segmented arm-guard on the sword-arm. The most famous Thracian was Spartacus, who led a gladiators' revolt against his Roman masters in 73 BC (see page 100).

THE *PROVOCATORES*

The *provocator* was a late Republican gladiator type. *Provocatores* were slightly unusual amongst foot gladiators because they were never matched against any other type of fighter. They are thought to have been professional soldiers by training as their armour was always based on that of contemporary legionaries. There is a very detailed bas-relief of the early Augustan period, now in the Baths of Diocletian at Rome, that shows two of these gladiators fighting. Each wears an early imperial Gallic legionary helmet, a breastplate held on by straps, and a greave on the left leg. They also have segmented lower arm-guards. One fighter carries an oval, semi-cylindrical shield and his opponent has a rectangular one. This mirrors exactly the situation in the first century BC, when both types of shield were in use in the legions before the rectangular type took over as the more popular weapon of defence. The gladiator with his back towards us rests his shield on the ground and holds back his right arm in the gesture of submission. The partial inscription IVL VVV (*Iulianus pugnarum V, coronarum V, vicit*) above the victorious *provocator* tells us that he came from the gladiator school founded by Julius Caesar at Capua, that this was his fifth fight and that he had been awarded the laurel crown in recognition of his exemplary performance in all five contests.

This bas-relief, which dates from the late first century BC, was found in a tomb in Rome and shows two *provocatores* fighting on the left and a *murmillo* on the right.

THE *VELITES*

Like the *provocatores*, the *velites* were also probably professional soldiers of the late Republican era and they too only ever fought each other in the arena. They were more lightly armed than most other types of gladiator and their weapon of choice was a javelin. This type disappears from the records shortly before the end of the second century BC.

THE *EQUITES*

The *equites* were horsemen and they were only ever paired off against each other. According to the Spanish archbishop Isidore of Seville (AD *c.* 560–636), the *equites* rode white horses and were usually scheduled to appear first at the afternoon gladiatorial contests. Many pictorial representations show them fighting on foot, which would indicate that they started off on horseback and then dismounted to finish the contest off. They can be identified from the type of shield that they carried – the small, round *parma equestris* – which they continued to use right through the imperial age. Other weapons and equipment associated with the *equites* changed over time as they adopted the visored helmets, greaves and segmented arm-guards worn by other types of gladiator.

There was a special type of *equites* known as the *andabatae*. These were heavily armoured cavalrymen, probably brought back to Rome from the eastern Mediterranean after the defeat of Antiochus the Great in 190 BC. According to the literary sources they wore visored helmets without eye-holes – rather a serious handicap, one would have thought, even if the horses were not blinkered.

GLADIATORS OF THE IMPERIAL AGE

By the middle of the first century BC the games had become an extremely important political and cultural element in Roman society. They were now no longer exclusively religious events held in honour of the dead but had been hijacked by the ruling elite for the purposes of propaganda. Gladiatorial contests were seen as a useful political tool that the wealthy exploited in order to display their power, to raise their profiles and to win votes. The early emperors in the first century AD were quick to stop them from gaining too much influence, however, and they soon took control of when

An early third-century AD mosaic from the town of Augusta Raurica (Augst) in Switzerland showing *equites* (identified from their tunics and round shields) who have dismounted from their horses and are continuing to fight on foot.

and where the contests were allowed to take place. And like a modern multinational company spending lavishly on corporate hospitality to impress their clients, the emperors put on a spectacular show and would offer ringside seats to foreign rulers and ambassadors just to let them know how mighty the Roman Empire was.

THE SECUTORES AND THE RETIARII

The most common gladiatorial pairing of the early imperial age was between the *secutor* and the *retiarius* – the pursuer and the pursued. The *secutor* was armed with a semi-cylindrical shield and the same type of sword as used by the legionaries. He wore a padded, segmented arm-guard and a short greave and what made him instantly identifiable was his helmet, which

This bronze statuette of
a *secutor* from Arles in
southern France was made
in the second century AD.

was egg-shaped and brimless with a short, plain metal crest and two very small eyeholes. His traditional opponent, the *retiarius*, was the lowest-ranking gladiator. He was immediately recognizable because he used a net and a trident (his name, in fact, is derived from *rete*, the Latin word for 'net'). There are a number of representations showing the *retiarius* holding his trident with two hands, the traditional stance being with the leading arm (usually the left one) thrust forward with the other arm held back, behind the body. Unfortunately, archaeologists have failed to find any examples of a complete trident or net, so we only have these contemporary illustrations to show us what they looked like. The trident, with its characteristic three-pronged head, appears in most cases to have been quite small.

The *retiarius* did not have a shield but he was permitted to carry a dagger or short sword. He wore very little body armour, being allowed a single arm-guard (the same type as the *secutor*), and a metal shoulder-guard (*galerus*). The shoulder-guard gave some protection to his throat and lower face but otherwise he went bare-headed and bare-legged. He was therefore quite exposed and vulnerable but at least he was not as heavily weighed down with armour as some other types of gladiator. (A bronze statuette of a *retiarius* with his trident from Esbarres in France is repro-duced on page 1.) The *retiarius* was generally reckoned to be the weaker opponent so it was important for him to be agile. His aim was either to goad or keep the *secutor* at a distance with the trident, to tangle and ensnare him in the net and then to finish him off with the dagger. The *secutor's* distinctive smooth helmet had no ridges, feather holders or raised decoration and this was a deliberate feature of the design, for it meant that the *retiarius's* net had nothing much to catch on.

The Roman poet and satirist Juvenal (AD *c.* 60–*c.* 140) confirms the poor status that the *retiarius* enjoyed and his descrip-tion of a young nobleman from the influ-ential Gracchus family who voluntarily chose to be one is wonderfully scornful:

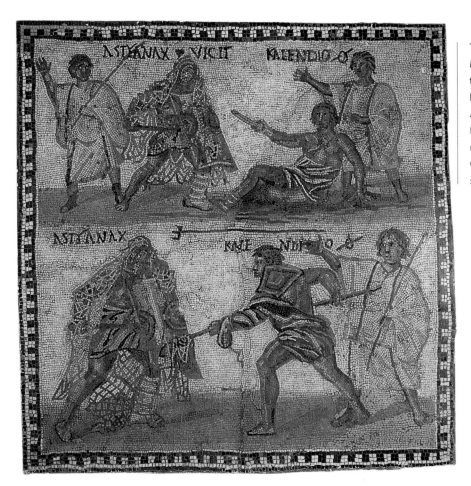

This mosaic in the Madrid Museum shows two phases of a contest between the *secutor* Astyanax and the *retiarius* Kalendio. Kalendio has netted his opponent. The Θ (*theta*) after his name shows that he was killed.

And in the gladiator school also you have seen scandal in our city: a Gracchus fighting, not indeed as a *murmillo*, nor with the round shield and curved sword: such accoutrements he rejects and detests; nor does a helmet hide his face. See what he wields – a trident! And when with poised right hand he has cast the trailing net in vain, he lifts up his bare face to the benches and flees for all to recognize from one end of the arena to the other. Look at his tunic, golden cord and fringe, and that odd conspicuous shoulder-guard.

THE *HOPLOMACHUS*

In sharp contrast to the *retiarius*, the *hoplomachus* was probably the most heavily armed and well protected of all the gladiators. And 'heavily armed' is what the word *hoplomachus* means in Greek, a term that is probably derived from *hoplite*, the name for a Greek infantryman.

This relief from the monument of Lusius Storax in the Chieti museum shows a group of three gladiators – two Thracians on either side of a *hoplomachus*.

The *hoplomachus* fought with the usual straight stabbing sword favoured by the *secutores* and defended himself with a small shield of the type associated with the Macedonian pikemen. He wore a large-crested helmet with a visor, a single thigh-length greave on one leg and a segmented arm-guard on the leading arm.

THE *MURMILLO*

This gladiator type may have evolved from the earlier Gallic types; prisoners of war who were made to fight as gladiators during the Roman Republic. Their name is taken from the Greek word for a type of fish (*murmuros*), and although there are contemporary descriptions of *murmillones* wearing a fish emblem on their helmets there is curiously little archaeological evidence to support this. The *murmillo* originally did battle with the *hoplomachus* or Thracian gladiators in matches designed to reflect the rivalry between the Greek east and the Roman west, but was later paired with the *retiarius*. In addition to the distinctive helmet, the *murmillo* carried a large rectangular shield (*scutum*) and wore protection on his right arm and left leg.

THE FORGOTTEN GLADIATORS

There were several other types of gladiator in the imperial age but because there are so few references to them in the records that survive very little is known about them.

The *crupellarius* was a very heavily armed Gallic gladiator – 'clad entirely in iron' according to Tacitus, who provides us with the only written description. Apparently the armour these gladiators wore was so heavy and cumbersome that they could not get up if they fell over. The *dimachaerus* crops up a few times in the literary sources but apart from a Greek name implying that he carried two swords, nothing else is known about this gladiator. The *laquerarius* is another little known type. His name seems to be derived from the Latin word *laqueus* meaning 'noose' and some scholars take this as an indication that he was a defensive type of fighter like the *retiarius* and used a lasso rather than a net. The *sagittarius* was an archer and he probably appeared in the wild animal hunts. Pictorial representations show him armed with a reflex bow similar to those used by auxiliaries in the Roman army.

The *essedarius* was a charioteer whose name is derived from *essedrum*, a light chariot of a type that Caesar and Claudius would have encountered in Britain and possibly the type that Boudicca would have used. Archaeological remains found in burial tombs in Britain have allowed these chariots to be reconstructed with some authenticity. Caesar gives a vivid description of British warriors standing on the yoke bars of their chariots as they charged into battle and then jumping off in order to fight. The Romans figured that this style of combat would make excellent entertainment for the arena, and after the Claudian conquest *essedarii* appeared regularly at the games.

FEMALE GLADIATORS

There are several references to female gladiators in the ancient literary sources and some epigraphical evidence, too. The writer Petronius (d. AD 66), who satirized Nero and his hangers-on, mentions a female chariot fighter, an *essedaria*, who must have been brought to Rome from Britain soon after the Claudian conquest.

Women fighters were generally despised or treated as a joke and they seem to have been exploited mainly for their novelty value. Domitian made women fight at night by torchlight and the ever-fawning poet Martial lauds another of his spectacles where women fought against dwarfs. Juvenal expresses the popular Roman view of female gladiators and mocks them:

> Why need I tell you of the purple wraps and the wrestling oils used by
> women? Who has not seen one of them striking the stake, piercing it
> through and through with the wooden sword, lunging at it with a shield,
> and going through the proper motions? – a matron truly qualified to blow
> a trumpet at the *floralia*! Unless indeed she is nursing some further
> ambition in her bosom, and is practising for the real arena. What
> modesty can you expect in a woman who wears a helmet, abjures her
> own sex, and delights in feats of strength? Yet she would not choose to be
> a man, knowing the superior joys of womanhood. What a fine thing for a

A bas-relief dating from the first or second century BC from Halicarnassus (Bodrum) in south-western Turkey showing two female gladiators called Amazon and Achillia.

husband at an auction of his wife's effects, to see her belt and arm-guards and plumes put up for sale, with a gaiter that covers her left leg; or if she fight another sort of battle, how charmed you will be to see your young wife disposing of her greaves! Yet these are women who find the thinnest of thin robes too hot for them; whose delicate flesh is chafed by the finest of silk tissue. See how she pants as she goes through her prescribed exercises; how she bends under the weight of her helmet; how big and coarse are the bandages which enclose her haunches; and then laugh when she lays down her arms and shows herself to be a woman.

Nero loved to see female gladiators and he even encouraged noblewomen to appear in the arena. (Tacitus severely criticized him for this.) Ever the cruel showman, Nero once organized a spectacle for the Armenian king, Tiridates, in AD 66; all the gladiators were Ethiopian and he sent women and children into the arena alongside the men.

There are two female gladiators represented on a marble relief from Halicarnassus (Bodrum in Turkey) dating from the first or second century AD. Named Amazon and Achillia, they would appear to be armed as *murmillones*, wearing a segmented arm-guard on the right arm and carrying the traditional rectangular legionary shield. The inscription says that they had been given their freedom. The rest is conjecture.

In AD 200 Emperor Septimius Severus passed a law banning female gladiators altogether.

CONDEMNED CRIMINALS

A small number of gladiators were condemned criminals who were allowed to take their chances in the arena instead of being executed. If the gladiator schools heard of a particularly fearless individual they would often try to recruit him but the authorities could impose conditions, such as a deadline on the man's life, which effectively meant that the death sentence was merely postponed. Some criminals were set up to be killed on their first appearance in the arena while others were given the opportunity to earn their freedom if they managed to stay alive for three years.

VOLUNTEER GLADIATORS

Although most of the gladiators in Rome were forced into the arena to fight, there were some who chose to do so voluntarily. Livy refers to this minority as the 'free men who put their life's blood up for sale'. They did not just risk their lives in the arena, they also gave up all their civil privileges, forfeiting the right to vote and hold public office; sometimes they were even denied the right to a traditional burial. They swore an oath before a tribune of the people and accepted a contract to appear for an agreed period of time.

It may seem surprising that anyone would volunteer for such a life but for some it was a simple matter of survival as even young men from a noble family could hit hard times. For others the attraction was the thrill of combat, the fame and the adoration of the crowd. It was a colossal gamble, of course, but then life in the Roman army could be just as brutal and dangerous.

When the emperor Septimius Severus removed all the Italians from the Praetorian Guard at the end of the second century AD, replacing them with less corrupt soldiers from the Rhine and Danube legions, many of them joined a gladiatorial school. Pompeian graffiti refer to several such free men by name – Quintus Petillius, Lucius Sempronius and Lucius Fabius – and a list discovered at Venosa in southern Italy includes 28 gladiators, nine of whom appear to be free men. We have here a genuine clue because only free men were listed by two names, a forename and a surname, whereas most of the other gladiators tended to have a single 'stage' name or nickname.

THE GLADIATOR FANATICS

It was often the women in Roman society who were responsible for building up the reputation of a particular gladiator. There is a graffito from Pompeii that refers to a Thracian gladiator called Celado as the heart-throb of his day. These female fans (*amorates*) often became totally starstruck. Juvenal tells the story of Eppia, a senator's wife. She ran off to Egypt with a gladiator who was not, apparently, the youngest or the most handsome of men. 'And what were the youthful charms that captivated Eppia?' is Juvenal's ironic comment. 'What did she see in him to allow herself to be called a she-gladiator?'

But women were not alone in their adoration of the gladiators, for the men had their protégés too. The fans fell into two broad categories: the *scutarii*, who supported gladiators armed with a large shield (*scutum*), and the *parmularii*, who supported gladiators who carried a small shield (*parma/parmula*). The emperors Caligula and Titus were *parmularii* and were well known for championing the Thracians. Suetonius tells us that Caligula so favoured them that he reduced the amount of armour their traditional opponents, the *murmillones*, were allowed to wear. There was one *murmillo*, named Columbus, who won his fight in spite of this handicap, ending up slightly wounded. Caligula was furious and had the poor man's wound rubbed with poison. Nero and Domitian, on the other hand, were *scutarii* and the *murmillones* were their favourite gladiators. On one occasion Nero gave the estates of a disgraced senator to a *murmillo* named Spiculus, while Domitian had a man thrown into the arena to be torn to pieces by dogs for suggesting that a Thracian gladiator was as good as a *murmillo*.

THE PLAYBOY GLADIATORS

Young men from the Roman nobility often played at being gladiators and they usually did so out of bravado and to show off. They tended not to go in for the rigorous training associated with the gladiator schools and most of the fights were rigged in their favour. In spite of the fact that various laws had been passed in the first century BC to restrict the rights and privileges of any senator or member of the equestrian class who performed in the arena, the practice continued. There were even some emperors who positively encouraged these exploits. It is alleged that 400 senators and 600 knights were sent into the arena in AD 57 to fight each other but as it was Nero who had ordered them to do so they presumably had no choice in the matter.

This bone knife handle carved in the form of a *secutor* and *retiarius* dates from the late third century AD and was found in Avenches, Switzerland.

Nero often liked to play at being a gladiator himself, but there was one emperor who did become a serious fighter in the arena and that was Commodus. He was only 18 years old when he succeeded his father, Marcus Aurelius, in AD 180. Commodus was never going to survive into a peaceful old age and he only made it to 31 before being killed off by his enemies. He was an over-the-top flamboyant character, a bisexual libertine and a despot. He would often parade around the arena in his purple imperial cloak and gold crown, brandishing a jewelled sword in his left hand. It is recorded that he was bearded and left-handed.

Coins struck during his lifetime (and at least one bust) show Commodus in the guise of Hercules, and he played up to this image, swanning around Rome dressed in a lion-skin and carrying a club. He took pride in his skills as a sword-fighter and marksman and never stopped boasting of his superior strength and courage. He was just the kind of larger-than-life emperor that Hollywood loves and it is no surprise that Ridley Scott decided to set his film *Gladiator* during Commodus's reign and to depict him as the cruel

Bust of Commodus
as Hercules.

but petulant archetype. The Roman historian Herodian (b. *c.* AD 175) could have been pitching him to a casting director when he described him in literally glowing terms:

Commodus was of a striking appearance, with a shapely body and a handsome, manly face; his eyes were burning and flashing; his hair was naturally fair and curly, and when he went out in the sunlight it gleamed with such brilliance that some people thought gold dust was scattered on it before public appearances, though others considered it supernatural and said that a heavenly halo was shining round his head.

Commodus would often go into the arena in the mornings to fight wild animals and then appear again in the afternoons as a gladiator. He trained as a *secutor* and often stayed in the gladiators' barracks and insisted on being paid the same daily wage as the men. Anecdotal evidence suggests that he didn't exactly risk his life when he went into the arena: Dio Cassius and Herodian both say that whenever he fought against wild animals he was careful never to make contact with them.

It is said that Commodus once decapitated a hundred ostriches in a single session, using arrows with crescent-shaped heads. (An account of this by the eighteenth-century English historian Edward Gibbon is presented in Appendix II.) During a 14-day event at the Colosseum in November or December AD 192 he had the arena fenced off into four sections and had an elevated walkway built above it; from the safety of this position he shot at the animals below with arrows. He single-handedly despatched a tiger, a hippopotamus and an elephant and, according to Cassius Dio, a hundred bears. A highly decorated tunnel, discovered beneath the arena at the end of the eighteenth century, is believed to have been constructed specially for his exclusive use during this event and may also have been the site of an early assassination attempt in AD 182 when his sister Lucilla arranged for her nephew to lie in wait for him there. Her plan failed and Commodus had the two conspirators executed.

Altogether Commodus claimed 620 victories in his chosen role as a *secutor*. In one of these contests his opponent, forgetting his imperial orders, disarmed the emperor and challenged him to continue the bout bare-fisted. Commodus refused and ordered the man out of the arena, his fate all too easily imagined.

Commodus's bloodthirsty behaviour made him many enemies, especially in the Senate. On one occasion in the arena, after he had taken the head off an ostrich with a single sword stroke, he strode across to the podium. Confronting a group of senators, he held up the bird's head in one hand and his bloody sword in the other, his smile scarcely veiling the threat in his eyes. He paid dear for this arrogant gesture. Word went round that he was planning to have two consuls elect killed and intended to take on the office himself on 1 January 193. Worse than that, he also planned to perform at the gladiatorial games on that day, which from everyone's point of view would have been an extremely provocative thing to do. A small clique that included one of his favourite concubines, a woman named Marcia, and the commander of the Praetorian Guard decided this was intolerable. On the evening of 31 December 192, while Commodus was staying at the Vectilian Villa, a gladiator school, in preparation for his appearance in the arena the next day, Marcia tried to poison him. He was sick but did not die so she and her cohorts summoned one of his wrestling partners, who finished the job and strangled him.

One of the consuls he had planned to assassinate was given the satisfaction of burying him without ceremony during the night. After that the Senate had all the public statues of Commodus destroyed and auctioned off his gladiatorial equipment. He was later rehabilitated: on the orders of his successor, Pertinax, his remains were transferred to the Mausoleum of Hadrian and about four years later Septimius Severus honoured him with deification.

THE LIFE OF A GLADIATOR

As the games became an established part of their cultural life the Romans began to devise strict rules and regulations relating to the gladiators and their behaviour in the arena. How the contests were organized and the size and type of weapons and armour the combatants used were all strictly regulated. And even though the losers in a fight were often killed or fatally injured some of these rules were introduced for safety reasons – nearly all the helmets had visors to protect the eyes, for instance. No-one wanted the fights to be too one-sided so it was in everyone's interests that the gladiators were well trained and well equipped.

Opposite
A *provocator's* helmet from Pompeii. This type of helmet was based on the current legionary helmet, the imperial Gallic type.

WEAPONS AND EQUIPMENT

Over 80 per cent of all the gladiatorial weapons and equipment on public display today, most of it in the Naples Museum, comes from Pompeii and Herculaneum, the two towns buried by the eruption of Vesuvius in AD 79, a year before the opening of the Colosseum. The excavation in 1766-67 of the gladiator barracks behind the large theatre at Pompeii uncovered a hoard that included 15 complete helmets, 16 greaves and three shoulder-guards, together with a number of shields and weapons. Earlier excavators investigating the ruins of Herculaneum at various times between 1738 and 1765 had found five helmets, three greaves and a shoulder-guard. Most of the pieces from both hauls are highly decorated and were therefore identified as gladiatorial parade armour. The remaining, plainer, pieces are assumed to be fighting equipment.

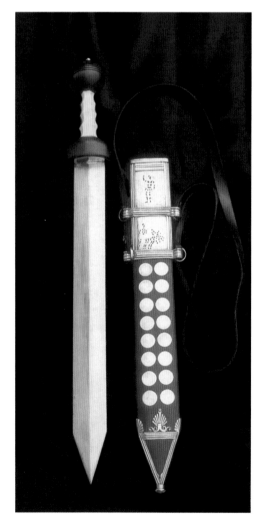

Modern reconstruction of a *secutor's* sword and its sheath.

The similarities between legionary and gladiatorial equipment in the imperial age is quite remarkable and at times it seems they were interchangeable. An unmodified legionary helmet, for example, was found in the amphitheatre at Arles in southern France and three legionary-type swords, identical to examples found on military sites in the Rhineland, were discovered at Pompeii.

WEAPONS

Swords used by *secutores*, *provocatores* and *murmillones* follow the development of the Roman legionary sword, the *gladius*. Before the reign of Augustus this was a long, pointed, cut-and-thrust sword with a 60-65-centimetre long blade. During the first half of the first century AD it gradually became shorter, and by the middle of the century it had been phased out to be replaced by a short, pointed sword with a blade length of 50 centimetres or less. Five of these have been found in Pompeii and are known as the 'Pompeii type'.

Thracians used the *sica*, a very short sword with a curved blade, a wooden example of which was discovered in the Roman fort at Oberaden in northern

Germany with a blade just over 30 centimetres long (refer to the illustration reproduced on page 108). This may well have been the *rudis* given to a Thracian gladiator on his retirement.

Three *retiarius'* daggers with bone handles were found at Pompeii. They have leaf-shaped iron blades varying from 19.5 centimetres to just under 30 centimetres in length.

No trident has been found, but the three-pointed heads were probably quite small.

SHIELDS

The shields used by gladiators reflect their origins. Gladiators from Italy –

A round shield of bronze inlaid with copper and silver found at Pompeii.

secutores, provocatores, murmillones and Samnites – normally used some form of the *scutum*, the Roman legionary shield. Originally oval in shape and semi-cylindrical so that it curved round the body giving greater protection, it was made of three layers of birchwood glued together in a similar way to plywood. It had a horizontal hand-grip and was covered inside and out with felt or hide. The *scutum* was reinforced by a long perpendicular boss in the shape of a spindle, the widest part of which covered the hand, and usually had a bronze or iron boss cover. Until the first century BC it was typically about 1.2 metres long. During the first century and possibly earlier, however, there was a rectangular version of roughly the same length. During the early empire the legions gradually changed over to a short-ened version of the rectangular shield that was about a metre in

Opposite
Four gladiator helmets
from Pompeii. Although
helmets with undulating
brims had a different
function from those with
flat brims, the two with a
griffin head on their crests
are usually identified as
Thracian helmets and
the other two as
murmillo helmets.

length. This change is reflected in the gladiators' shields: Thracians used a much smaller version of the *scutum* about 60 centimetres long.

The *equites* used the *parma equestris*, a type of shield employed by the Roman cavalry in the third and second centuries BC. It was round with a diameter of about 60 centimetres and slightly dished with a round boss in the centre, reinforcing the hand grip. It may have been made in the same way as the legionary shield. The *hoplomachus* had a similar shield but without a boss, probably derived from the Macedonian shield and made of wood with a bronze facing. Several of these have been found; they are often very small.

HELMETS

Gladiators' helmets fall into four main types – two with brims and two without. One of the brimless types is so distinctive that all examples are immediately identifiable as *secutores'* helmets. The second brimless type is harder to classify but the German historian Marcus Junkelmann has identified those in the Naples collection as *provocatores'* helmets.

With brimmed helmets it is far more difficult to discover which type of gladiator would have worn them. The main difference between them is that one type has a flat brim and the other has an undulating brim. A flat brim protected the wearer only from blows coming from above whereas an undulating brim gave further protection against a sideways slash. One could reasonably expect each type of brimmed helmet to be used by a different type of gladiator, for example a Thracian or a *murmillo*, but the only way they can be distinguished is by the shape of the crest and the emblems used for decoration.

The finest example in the Naples collection of the flat-brimmed type of helmet has a crest that curves forward, terminating in a griffin head. It is generally considered to be a Thracian helmet but apart from the shape of its crest and its decoration it is identical to another helmet that has a wedge-shaped crest and is therefore identified as that of a *murmillo*.

When comparing two of the helmets with undulating brims in the Naples collection things start to get confusing. Like the two flat-brimmed helmets, one has been declared a Thracian helmet and the other one a *murmillo* helmet, purely on the basis of the type of crest they have. If these identifications are correct then one can only assume that by AD 79 this kind of protective headgear was merely fancy dress and gladiator types could be identified only by their crests.

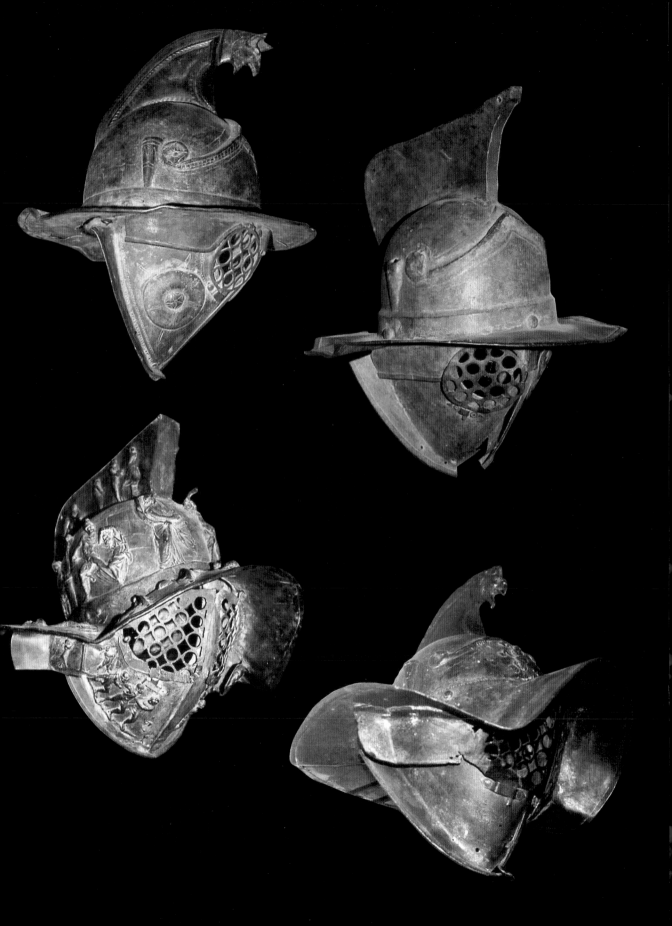

Exploded drawing of a *secutor's* bronze helmet from Herculaneum. This type of helmet was specifically designed to avoid becoming caught up in the *retiarius's* net.

Brimless Helmets: Type 1

There is a *secutor's* helmet from Herculaneum held by the Naples Museum that is in almost pristine condition. It is made entirely of bronze, constructed from several pieces joined together, and is characteristically smooth and egg-shaped. The skull and neck-guard are made in one piece. The crest, composed of two pieces joined along the upper edge, was made separately and appears to have been soldered or braised on. There are two cheek-pieces, hinged in the conventional way with the central leaf riveted to the skull and the top of the cheek-piece rolled over the hinge-pin. The cheek-pieces are reinforced on each side with a thick strip of bronze covering their junction with the skullcap, which would have given added protection to the nose, eyes and ears. The left cheek-piece, which has a thick central reinforcing strip riveted to its front edge, overlaps the right cheek-piece. Both cheek-pieces have a short flange, which fits into a bracket riveted to the skullcap. (The exploded drawing shows how the helmet was assembled.)

The angled flange at the bottom of the cheek-pieces would have protected the wearer's throat and the back of his neck against the *retiarius's* trident. The crescent-shaped crest, together with the elliptical perimeter of the neck-guard that continues along the bottom edge of the cheek-pieces, would have ensured that there was no protruding angle for his opponent's net to catch on. As the helmet is heavily reinforced around the eyes the wearer's range of vision would have been restricted and this would have been quite a handicap. A person can normally scan an area within a range of about 150 degrees (and be conscious of movement beyond this), without moving the head. This particular *secutor's* helmet would have reduced his range to an absolute limit of 50 degrees and this would have given a skilled *retiarius* an enormous advantage.

There are a further two examples of a *secutor's* helmet in the Naples collection, both from Pompeii and both rather damaged. The first is made of iron with some bronze fittings. The cheek-pieces operate in the same manner as the bronze Herculaneum example. The left cheek-piece has an iron reinforcing strip along the front edge. This originally covered the junction of the two cheek-pieces and slotted into a socket just below the crest of the helmet. The second example, made of bronze, appears to have worked in a similar way, though it is too corroded to tell.

A very noticeable feature of this type of helmet is the very restrictive nature of the cheek-pieces, which have horizontal reinforcing plates along the top, allowing them to move through no more than about 20 degrees – just enough for the wearer to get his head in. This compares with the cheek-pieces of a normal helmet, which are designed to rotate through 180 degrees.

Brimless Helmets: Type 2

The second brimless type of helmet is remarkable as it is clearly derived from the standard legionary helmet (with an added visor) current in the second half of the first century AD. It has a reinforcing brace across the forehead and three slightly raised ridges across the base of the neck. The legionary helmet had evolved from a Celtic prototype on which these ridges were much more pronounced so as to break the force of a blow glancing off the top of the helmet and sliding down the back of it. Two such helmets were discovered at Pompeii (one of these is illustrated on page 88) and one at Herculaneum and all three are elaborately decorated. A fourth example, consisting of an undecorated but very battered skullcap, is in the British Museum collection. All the Naples examples have a thick reinforcing strip extending from the end of the brow section to the leading edge of the neck-guard. This implies yet again that these helmets were designed to withstand heavy downward blows even though many contemporary illustrations of gladiators show them thrusting rather than cutting.

The cheek-pieces of these *provocatores'* helmets are actually enclosed within the neck of the helmet so they can hardly have opened at all. They close in the same way as the *secutores'* helmets, slotting into a bracket above the nose. All the elements of the visor cheek-piece assemblage are attached directly to the helmet skull. Even the side guards are riveted directly to it and this would have restricted the way in which the helmet could open even more.

Exploded drawing of a gladiator's bronze, flat-brimmed helmet from Pompeii.

Brimmed Helmets: Type 1

The flat-brimmed type of helmet clearly evolved from a late Hellenistic type used by Greek and Roman cavalrymen in the second to first century BC. A well-preserved example from Naples has the same characteristics, with ridges on a flat rim and a dart-shaped ridge splaying downwards from the centre of the brow. This helmet, which is made of bronze, is totally functional, with no decorative features whatsoever, and it was designed as a defence against an opponent armed with a downward-striking slashing weapon. There are visible cut marks on the volute (the spiral decoration above the ear), suggesting that the helmet had been used in combat. The volute is an important feature of the design because it helps to absorb the force of a blow, and the dart-shaped ridge is there to deflect it from the upper part of the forehead. Below the volute is a ridge extending all the way around the helmet that serves to strengthen it and also helps to break the force of a blow. The brim, which must ultimately stop the blow, is reinforced by changes of plane. Rather like corrugated iron, it is far more difficult to bend something shaped in this way than flat metal.

Just above the point where the skull of the helmet turns out to form the brim there are three large rivets, one at each side and one in the middle above the nose. These secure a strip of bronze stretching around the inside of the front half of the helmet. All the elements of the visor and cheek-pieces are riveted to this strip. In the centre the strip protrudes downwards to cover the top of the nose. A socket holding the cheek-pieces together is riveted onto this. Above each ear the end of the strip extends outwards to form a flange just below the brim. These flanges secure the rear end of reinforcing strips covering the upper part of the cheek-pieces. The other ends are held in place by the rivets of the socket above the nose. Two grilles, hinged at the top and with small tongues at the bottom slotting into brackets on the cheek-pieces, protect the eyes. These would have to be fitted as the cheek-pieces were closing and the wearer would have needed the assistance of another person to do this. The lower part of the cheek-pieces turns outwards to deflect blows away from the neck. This feature is common to virtually all gladiator helmets, as is the vertical reinforcing strip covering the nose and mouth. Towards the bottom of the right-hand cheek-piece is a narrow slot cut into the inside edge. This probably fitted behind a raised pin on the inside of the other cheek-piece, ensuring that the two cheek-pieces were correctly aligned.

Brimmed Helmets: Type 2

The second type of brimmed helmet has a broad, undulating rim giving it a bonnet-like appearance. No fewer than eight of these were found at Pompeii. They are all elaborately decorated. The cheek-piece and visor unit close in a somewhat different way to the flat-brimmed kind. There is no bracket above the nose. Instead the prongs of the cheek-pieces pass through holes in the brim of the helmet and are pinned in position. The eye-guards are not hinged at the top but have a tongue that fits into a small hole in the brim. The side guards on all these helmets are riveted to the brim of the helmet. A very well-preserved example of an undulating brimmed helmet with no raised decoration is in the collection of the British Museum. Its provenance is unknown but it is fundamentally the same as the Naples helmets (though made up of a few more individual pieces) and of the same date. The skull and neck-guard are made separately and the neck-flange at the bottom edge of the cheek-piece, also made separately, is riveted on. The reinforcing strip that would normally cover the junction of the two cheek-pieces is on the inside of the helmet. A locking device at the bottom of the cheek-piece seems to be a great improvement on the Naples examples. The undulating brim on the helmet gave the wearer greater protection to the side of the face whilst allowing maximum visibility.

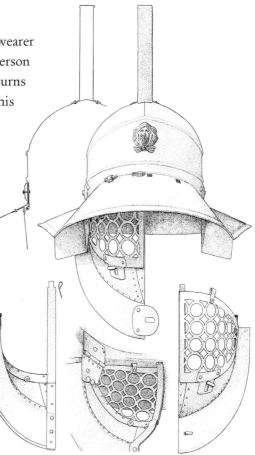

Exploded drawing of a gladiator's bronze helmet with an undulating brim. The original helmet is held by the British Museum.

BODY ARMOUR

Breastplates

Very few gladiators wore breastplates. Most fought with a bare torso, their most vulnerable spot. *Provocatores* shown on the bas-relief in the Baths of Diocletian at Rome (see page 75) wear a short breastplate covering the chest and occasionally shirts of mail or scale are shown, as on the Munich bas-relief (see page 131), but it is unusual. No actual example has yet been found.

Greaves

The Thracian and *hoplomachus* both wore thigh-length greaves attached by three straps. The *murmillo* is sometimes shown wearing thigh-length greaves and at other times only shin-guards. Ten bronze thigh-length greaves were found at Pompeii. All except one pair of these are decorated to some degree,

A full-length greave (*left*) and a *secutor's* shin guard found at Herculaneum.

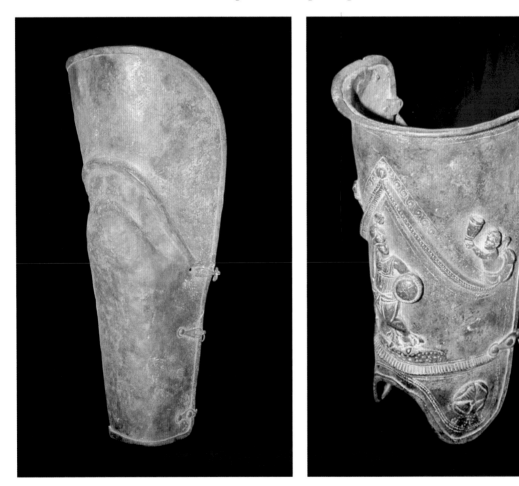

some with complex figural scenes in high relief. The undecorated pair is beautifully made, being moulded to fit the muscular contours of the leg. All the examples found have a pronounced raised ridge at the lower thigh to deflect blows away from the knee. Those discovered at Pompeii vary in length from 48 to 58 centimetres and are very broad at mid-thigh level to allow for padding and ease of movement. Ancient authors often refer to this thick padding, which was attached to the leg and not the greave.

The *secutor* always wore a short shin-guard, nine bronze examples of which were found at Pompeii and Herculaneum. Like the thigh-length greaves, most of these are highly decorated. (Only one, from Herculaneum, is without decoration, and may be part of the same equipment as the *secutor* helmet mentioned above.) These shin-guards vary in length from 28 to 35 centimetres and are held in place by two or three straps. All have a shallow dome raised over the ankle, and about half of those found have a raised horizontal ridge just above the foot which was intended to break the force of a trident sliding down the greave. The dimensions of these short greaves show that they were worn over very thick padding, which was probably made of linen. This can be seen on many pictorial representations.

Arm-Guards

Marcus Junkelmann argues that the metal arm-guards did not exist and that the arm-guards shown on mosaics, which are usually white or grey, were in fact fabric padding strapped to the arm. It is true that no arm-guards were found among the gladiator armour discovered at Pompeii and Herculaneum but these were very early excavations akin to treasure hunts, and small strips of metal from segmented arm-guards may have been discarded as being of no value. Bearing in mind the constant interchange of armour and weapons between soldiers and gladiators, Junkelman's argument seems difficult to sustain, as many metal arm-guards have been found on Roman military sites. Furthermore, many bronze pieces of armour were tinned and it is not known what percentage of armour was made of iron. In both cases these would be shown as white or grey.

Shoulder-Guards

All four known surviving shoulder-guards (*galeri*) come from the Naples area, three from Pompeii and one from Herculaneum. The surviving examples are made of bronze, but it seems certain that all examples of gladiator

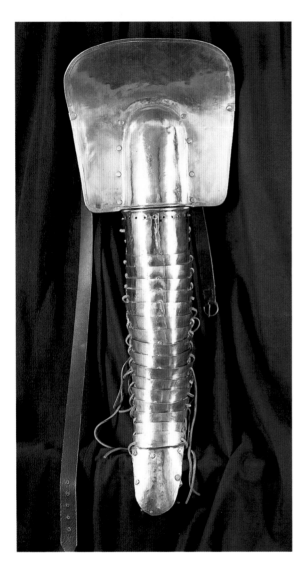

Modern reconstruction of a shoulder-guard (*galerus*) and a segmented arm-guard of a *retiarius*.

armour were also made of iron. The Herculaneum piece is the simplest and best-preserved example. The upper part is strongly curved forward to deflect blows down onto the well-defended shoulder. It has two pairs of ring fasteners on the back. The lower of these must have secured it to the arm and the upper ones secured a leather strap passing round the neck or across the chest. These straps are shown on many contemporary illustrations.

THE GLADIATOR TRAINING SCHOOLS

The earliest and most renowned gladiator training schools (*ludi*) were established not in Rome but in Capua, the chief city in Campania. Aemilius Scaurus set up the first private gladiator training school there in the second century BC. These schools were privately run and their proprietors grew rich as the games became more popular. They functioned like a combination of military barracks and prisons as most of the men there were not free, being slaves, prisoners of war or criminals. The conditions they were kept in were harsh. When Pompeii was excavated archaeologists uncovered the skeletons of several gladiators wearing leg shackles. The room they were found in had such a low ceiling that the men would not have been able to stand upright.

SPARTACUS

It was from a gladiator training school in Capua, owned by Lentulus Batiatus, that the most famous gladiator of all, a Thracian called Spartacus, led a revolt in 73 BC. What began as a minor protest developed into a massive revolt as thousands of slaves and farm workers flocked to join him. The rebels first established a camp on the slopes of Vesuvius and the Romans sent the praetor Gaius Claudius Glaber to put the mutiny down. He was attacked by the gladiators and defeated, as were further praetorian armies. With renewed strength and confidence, Spartacus and his followers, now a formidable contingent of some 70,000 men, marched out and started pillaging the countryside.

One of Spartacus's main supporters, Oenomaus, was killed during one of the early skirmishes, and another, Crixus, was defeated with part of the rebel army near the promontory of Gargano in the far southeast of Italy. This left Spartacus in sole command. He moved up the Adriatic coast with his army, intending to cross the Alps into neutral territory. He was pursued by two Roman consular armies and when he reached the Po valley he found himself face to face with a third, led by the proconsul Longinus. Spartacus changed his plans and headed south again, cutting a swath through the Roman armies as he went. He headed for Lucania in southern Italy, followed by the Roman general Crassus, who was supported by six legions – some 25,000 men. Crassus finally managed to drive Spartacus right down into the 'toe' of Italy and spent a whole winter building a rampart and ditch across the peninsula to keep him there. Spartacus tried to break through this barrier twice but failed and suffered heavy losses. He succeeded on the third attempt but Crassus and his men caught up with him. Spartacus allegedly killed two centurions before he was cut down. (His body was never found.) The surviving rebels fled to the hills. Those that were caught were dealt with severely – Crassus reportedly had 6000 of them crucified on crosses set up at regular intervals along the Appian Way, the road that linked Capua to Rome.

Rome had learned a hard lesson: keeping large numbers of gladiators pent up together in one place was asking for trouble. The Senate limited the number of men staying in the capital and dispersed the rest to Capua and other towns in Campania. But the ruling elite were not about to abolish the gladiators, for they knew just how useful they were, first of all as a commodity – they were bought and sold just like the slaves but were worth considerably more – and secondly as a means of wooing the electorate.

Plan of the area to the east of the Colosseum showing the positions of the various *ludi*. Most of these have been identified from the *Forma Urbis Romae*, the second-century marble plan of Rome.

A Ludus Dacicus

B Castra Misenatium

C Ludus Magnus

D Armamentaria

E Ludus Matutinus

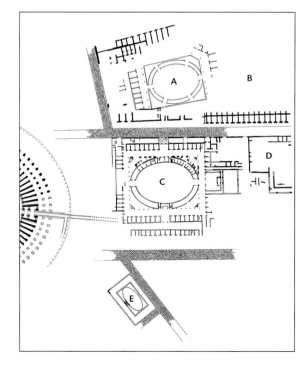

TRAINING SCHOOLS IN ROME

By the end of the first century AD the focus of gladiator training had shifted from Capua to Rome and four main schools were established there: Ludus Magnus, Ludus Dacicus, Ludus Gallicus and Ludus Matutinus. As far as we know they were all established during the reign of Domitian (AD 81–96) and they would have accommodated around two thousand gladiators between them at any one time.

According to surviving fragments of the Severan marble plan of Rome, the *Forma Urbis Romae* dating from the second century AD, which showed every street and building that existed at the time, the Ludus Dacicus was situated immediately to the north of the Ludus Magnus on the opposite side of the Via Labicana. It was about the same size as the Ludus Magnus, and gets its name from the Dacians, the Danubian people who fought the Romans during the reigns of both Domitian and Trajan. To the south of the Ludus Magnus, again of a similar size, was the Ludus Matutinus (also known as the Ludus Bestiarius) and this is where the animal fighters lived and trained. The name 'Matutinus' means 'of the morning', and this refers to the fact that the animal hunts usually took place in the mornings. There is nothing left today to show where the Ludus Gallicus was but it is believed to have been next door to the Ludus Matutinus and was named after the Gauls, the traditional Celtic enemies of Rome.

The Castra Misenatium, named after the Roman naval base at Misenum in the Bay of Naples, was where the marines who were responsible for the awnings of the Colosseum lived. The building was situated to the north of the Via Lubicana. The gladiators' weapon store (*armamentaria*) was south of this.

Ludus Magnus

As the name suggests, the Ludus Magnus was the main gladiator school in Rome. The construction is of brick-faced concrete throughout and the building was started by Domitian and completed some time during the reign of Hadrian. It was situated right next to the Colosseum, on the east side, and the two buildings were connected by a 60-metre underground passageway. Its precise location was uncertain until 1937, although its layout was partially known from the *Forma Urbis Romae*.

The main entrance of the Ludus Magnus was on the north side, where a wide staircase led down from the Via Labicana. This gave onto a large

Opposite
Cut-away section of the Ludus Magnus with the Colosseum in the background. The small training area in the centre is surrounded by offices and living quarters.

Part of the excavated remains of the Ludus Magnus today.

rectangular courtyard surrounded by porticoes. Behind these was a series of rooms, 14 on the longer sides and ten on the shorter. It is thought that the building was probably three storeys high with up to 144 rooms altogether. The courtyard functioned like an amphitheatre and this was where the gladiators did their training. There was an arena in the middle that measured 63 × 42 metres and this was surrounded by a wall 2 metres high, topped by a cornice of white marble. There were entrances at the ends of the main east–west axis and four more on the curves, two on each side. A narrow *cavea*, only just over 6 metres wide, was supported on a series of vaulted substructures, which were divided into underground rooms that were accessible only from the arena. One of these rooms was a latrine and it is believed that the others were used for storage.

The *cavea* was large enough to hold eight or nine terraces and had room for up to 3000 spectators.

RUNNING THE SCHOOLS

Each gladiator training school was headed by a procurator who was appointed directly by the emperor. This person was usually a member of the equestrian class (the class below the senatorial class) and he was responsible for the finances and general administration of the school. He managed a large staff of experts, including trainers, medics, masseurs, armourers, security guards, accountants and scribes. Each gladiator belonged to a specific group or troupe (*familia gladiatoria*) belonging to a chief trainer known as a *lanista* (a word of Etruscan origin that would support the theory that gladiators came originally from Etruria). From the time of the first Roman emperor, Augustus, the *lanista* was directly accountable to the sovereign and it was one of his main tasks to make sure that there was always a fresh supply of trained gladiators graduating from the school. He was like a talent scout, and he would go to the slave auctions to bid for the fittest men he could find. The major gladiator schools, such as those at Rome and Capua, had specialist instructors (*doctores*) in the different forms of combat. Many of these are known from inscriptions such as *doctor retiariorium, doctor secutorum, doctor Thraecorum*, etc.

Galen

One of the founding fathers of modern medicine, and the author of numerous works on anatomy and physiology, was the Greek physician Galen (AD 129-199). He spent the last part of his life in Rome as chief physician at the imperial court, treating, among others, Marcus Aurelius, Commodus and Septimius Severus, but as a young man he was attached to the gladiator school in Pergamum (Bergama). He was there for four years, from AD 157 to 161, during which time he gained a great deal of his practical experience and knowledge from treating the gladiators in his care. He said that wounds were 'windows into the body' and claimed that his skill allowed him to reduce the gladiators' mortality rate quite considerably. As well as treating their injuries he also advised on their diet, which was inclined to be nourishing rather than tasty. Barley soup was recommended but Galen criticized the practice of mixing it with beans, saying that they made the muscles soft.

Basic Training

Exactly how long a gladiator's basic training lasted is not known, but it was generally reckoned to be a brutal regime. But at least the strict discipline produced fighters who had superior combat skills and self-control, and it was these qualities that gave them the greatest chance of staying alive in the arena. When they were training they were initially given heavier weapons than normal in order to toughen them up and strengthen their muscles. These methods were so well-respected that the army adopted the same techniques. In AD *c.* 400 the Roman writer Vegetius described the gladiatorial training practices adopted by the legions in 105 BC:

> A stake was planted in the ground by each recruit, in such a manner that
> it projected six feet in height and could not sway. Against this stake the
> recruit practised with his wickerwork shield and wooden stave just as
> if he were fighting a real enemy. Sometimes he aimed against the head
> or face, sometimes he threatened the flanks, sometimes he endeavoured
> to strike down at the knees and legs. He gave ground, he attacked, he
> assaulted and he assailed the stake with all the skill and energy required
> in actual fighting, just as if it were a real enemy; and in this exercise care
> is taken to see that the recruit did not rush forward so rashly to inflict
> a wound as to lay himself open to a counterstroke from any quarter.

Once a novice had finished his initial training he became a *tiro* and he only needed to win one fight to became a veteran (*veteranus*). A novice would not normally be matched against a veteran but would usually face an opponent of similar experience. This was not necessarily because of any sense of fairness on the part of the organizers of the *munera* or the *lanistas*. The former would want to give the crowds their money's worth – like the spectators at a modern boxing match, Roman audiences would have felt cheated by short, uneven contests that failed to entertain – and the latter would be reluctant to waste all the time and money it had taken to train the fighter in the first place. However, there are one or two recorded examples of a *tiro* being matched against a veteran. One of the graffiti from Pompeii records a fight between a veteran Thracian named Hilarus with 14 victories and a novice *murmillo* called Attilius. Incredibly, Attilius won, though Hilarus survived. Attilius went on to defeat another Thracian, Lucius Raecius Felix, who had twelve victory crowns. He lived, too.

A GLADIATOR'S CAREER

The *lanista* decided what style of fighting would most suit the new recruits, depending on their age and physical condition. A lithe, agile youth might train as a *retiarius*, the man with the net and trident, while a bigger, more muscular man might be selected for training as a heavy-armed *hoplomachus*. Some exceptional gladiators were skilled in two different techniques.

On enrolment, a gladiator had to swear an oath of obedience. Exactly how this was worded is not known but the Roman writer Petronius (d. AD 66) tells us what it amounted to in his sharply observed account of Roman society, *Satyricon*: 'We solemnly swear to obey [the *lanista*] in everything. To endure burning, imprisonment, flogging and even death by the sword.' A gladiator's contract included an agreed length of service, assuming he lasted that long.

A *tiro* was allowed to choose his own fighting name. Some gladiators went for something relating to their superior strength and ferocity: Invictus (Invincible), Ferox (Ferocious), Leo (Lion), Tigris (Tiger), and some adopted the persona of a mythical hero, such as Hector, Diomedes, Ajax, Hercules or Perseus; others took names that described their appearance or performance such as Ursius (bear-like) or Callidromus (speedy). For some reason, perhaps to appeal to the women, some chose the names of precious stones, such as Pearl, Beryl or Amethyst. Many of these names are known from inscriptions and graffiti. The first gladiators mentioned by name appear in a fragment of the writings of Lucilius:

> In a public show given by the Flacci was a certain Aeserninus, a Samnite,
> a nasty fellow worthy of that life and station. He was matched with
> Pacideianus, who was by far the best of all gladiators since the creation
> of man.

Although the Colosseum was the most important of all the gladiatorial arenas, there was always plenty of scope for a fighter away from Rome. Many of them lived an itinerant life, moving from place to place in groups. One inscription tells of a *retiarius* named Rapidus, who trained at the school in Aquileia at the north end of the Adriatic, toured the amphitheatres of northern Italy and down the east coast of the Adriatic. He fought at Bellunum and Como and died from wounds received in a fight at the amphitheatre at Salona in modern Croatia.

Drawing of the wooden *sica*, a curved dagger used by Thracian gladiators, found at Oberaden in northern Germany, which may have been given to a Thracian gladiator on his retirement.

If a gladiator survived long enough to complete his contract he was allowed to retire from active combat and he became a freedman. If he wished he could continue to fight as a freelance but more often than not he would become a trainer or a referee. On the completion of his contract a surviving gladiator was awarded a wooden sword (*rudis*) and, according to his ability, the title of 'second sword' (*secunda rudis*) or 'top sword' (*summa rudis*). These honours entitled him to become a second-class or first-class referee. The highest award that could be given to a gladiator was the title of *primus palus* (*palus* being the stake against which they practised fighting) and this was analogous to the title of *primus pilus*, which was the highest rank of centurion in a legion. Some *primi pali* became masters in the use of certain specific weapons. At the time of the opening of the Colosseum they were freelance, offering their services wherever there was a demand, but later they became professional teachers with the status of freedmen in the employ of the emperor.

When a gladiator died in the arena he was carried to the *spoliarium*, which was a bit like a morgue, where his armour was removed. It is not known whether the Colosseum had its own *spoliarium* or whether the gladiator training schools each had their own. We do know from an inscription that there was a *curator spoliarii* at the Ludus Matutinus, where the animal hunters lived. Unlike the criminals and martyrs, whose bodies were often mutilated and dumped after they were executed, most gladiators appear to have been given a proper burial. Sometimes specific terms relating to their funeral arrangements were included in their contracts and some gladiators belonged to a burial club or guild, just as the Roman craftsmen did, which ensured that there was enough money to bury them properly. Many of the successful, established gladiators, especially those who had retired and achieved free status, would have been rich enough to provide the funds for their own funerals and an expensive engraved tombstone.

In spite of the obvious risks involved in being a gladiator, it is surprising how many men did survive into retirement, some of them after very long and active careers. A lot of the information about their lives and achievements comes from their tombstones, which list not only their victories and awards (crowns) but sometimes even the fights that ended in a draw. Some note that the dead gladiator had been left-handed (*scaeva*), which was a novelty that the crowds appreciated. Graffiti also add a little to our knowledge, as with the following example from Pompeii:

Pugnax, a Thracian of the Neronian Ludus, with three fights to his
credit – victorious; Murrans, a *murmillo* of the Neronian Ludus, with
three fights – killed; Cycnus, a *hoplomachus* of the Julian Ludus,
with eight fights – victorious; Atticus, a Thracian with 14 fights –
reprieved.

One free man, Publius Ostorius, notched up 51 fights according to another
graffito at Pompeii. An inscription on the tombstone of a gladiator called
Maximus, who was attached to the imperial school at Capua, states that
he won 40 fights and received 36 crowns. One from Nîmes in France tells
us that the gladiator Faustus won 37 fights, and another dedicated to a
Florentine called Urbicus, a *secutor*, records that he had fought 13 times
before he was killed, probably at the age of 32, and had received the titles
secundus and *primus palus*. He left a wife and two daughters, who had
shared his spartan life in the gladiator barracks. He may well have been
killed by a *retiarius* whose life he had previously spared, for his wife added
a few words of warning to others at the bottom of his tombstone: 'I advise
you to kill whoever you have defeated.'

As the odds shortened with age some gladiators tried to renegotiate
the terms of their contract and retire early. Suetonius mentions a chariot
fighter who was awarded the wooden sword by Claudius personally after
the man's four sons begged the emperor to discharge him. And others tried
to prolong their time in the arena. Like many a modern ageing star, there
were some gladiators who made more than one comeback. It is alleged that
Tiberius had to pay a thousand gold pieces to persuade certain popular
veterans to return to the arena.

IN THE ARENA

The gladiatorial games in ancient Rome were a bit like modern football matches. The events were well organized, with league tables, a system of betting, powerful bosses, managers and trainers whose livelihood depended on winning, superstar players and fanatical supporters. Victory was everything and there was a serious price to pay for failure. Contests between gladiators were only one of many forms of entertainment held in the amphitheatre, however. Support acts included the staged hunting and slaughter of wild animals, comedy warm-up acts and public executions *ad bestias* of criminals – including early Christians.

Opposite
Detail from one of the Borghese mosaics showing a staged animal hunt.

WILD ANIMALS

Before the gladiators made an appearance in the arena it was customary to treat the audience to a series of shows involving wild animals. In the very early days these creatures were merely paraded or displayed in cages as if in a zoo and the crowd would be content just to look at them. The mock hunts and wholesale slaughter came later.

Exotic animals arrived in Rome as a direct consequence of the expansion of the empire. Capturing new species was always part of any planned expedition overseas, and the Roman army employed specially trained people for the job. The eastern Mediterranean produced lions, tigers and hippopotamuses while North Africa provided elephants, rhinoceroses, leopards (panthers), lynxes, giraffes, monkeys, camels, antelopes, horses, wild asses, crocodiles and ostriches. Bulls came from Greece, and bears, bison and the aurochs were imported from northern Europe. Apart from wolves, deer, goats, wild boar and wild cats, Italy appears to have had few creatures of its own to exploit in the arena.

Demand for animals continued as the Romans settled the areas they had conquered. Provincial administrators, especially those stationed along the north coast of Africa, were constantly being urged to keep up the supply.

There is one mosaic from Hippo in North Africa that shows the capture of lions and leopards. There is an area enclosed on three sides by nets, concealed behind bushes. This is baited with gazelles, sheep, goats and other domestic animals to lure the prized wild beasts in. Once they have been trapped inside the netted area men with torches and shields drive the animals towards a cart. This is somewhat similar to a modern horsebox, with a vertical sliding door at the back. The dangerous nature of the operation is illustrated with the scene of a leopard mauling a hunter who has fallen on the ground. The mosaic also shows ostriches and in the top right-hand corner there is a hunter on horseback lassoing a wild ass.

Another mosaic, known as the 'Great Hunt', from the Villa del Casale in Piazza Armerina in Sicily, dating from the fourth century AD, has representations of lions, tigers, leopards, bison, rhinoceroses, hippopotamuses, elephants, giraffes, bulls, antelopes, wild boar and ostriches. Some of the animals are shown being prepared for loading into high-sided ox-drawn wagons, and one scene illustrates how they were then put onto ships, the small animals, such as antelopes and ostriches, being carried aboard, while

the bigger ones are driven up the gangplank. Pliny the Elder once saw some elephants being disembarked at Pozzuoli near Naples. The animals had been pushed to the back of the ship but were too terrified to step out onto the gangplank. In the end they had to be turned round and escorted onto the quayside backwards.

Some of the ships from Africa would have landed at Ostia, a port situated at the mouth of the River Tiber. The animals would then have been transferred to smaller vessels and ferried up-river to Rome. There is a sarcophagus in the Villa Medici at Rome with decoration showing a ship under sail. On the deck there are lions in three wooden cages.

Elephants had been known to the Romans since 275 BC when four of the Indian type were seized during a battle with King Pyrrhus at Beneventum. Marcus Curius Dentatus exhibited them in his triumph. More elephants, this time captured from the Carthaginians in Sicily, reached Rome in 252 BC and again in 197 BC. These were a species of small elephant that came from North Africa but is now extinct.

STAGED ANIMAL HUNTS

The first recorded show involving wild animals was arranged by Marcus Fulvius Nobilior, who presented lions and leopards to the public in the Circus Maximus in 187 BC. Within 20 years all sorts of animals, including bears and elephants, were being sent into the arena to be slaughtered by the thousand. Animal hunts (*venationes*) became an official part of state

This mosaic from Hippo in North Africa shows the capture of exotic animals for the amphitheatre. Gazelles, sheep, goats and other domestic animals in pens act as bait. A camouflaged net has been set up around them to trap the wild beasts, which are driven in by armed men on horseback and on foot, one of whom has fallen and is being attacked by a leopard.

This mosaic from the Villa del Casale in Piazza Armerina in Sicily dates from the fourth century AD and shows animals destined for the arena being loaded onto a ship. Two men in the background are carrying a wild boar in a net.

festivals in 169 BC when Publius Lentulus and Scipio Nasica organized an event involving 63 leopards and 40 bears plus an unknown number of elephants in the Circus Maximus.

With typical Roman showmanship, the organizers would dream up ingenious ways of using the animals at their disposal in various permutations. They wanted to entertain the crowds so they offered them variety, novelty, the element of surprise and danger, the gory outcome. The Romans enjoyed watching not only men fighting animals but also animals fighting animals. There is a record of full-scale elephant fights being staged in the Circus Maximus in 99 BC. Elephants were always popular, presumably because they were the biggest and heaviest beasts available. And they were not just pitted against each other: sometimes they were matched against bulls.

When Pompey marched his troops across the Middle East in 66-62 BC, annexing Syria and creating vassal states in Palestine and Egypt, he sent a hippopotamus and five crocodiles back to Rome, where they were exhibited in a special pool. To celebrate the opening of his new theatre he chose a hippopotamus, a lynx, elephants and Ethiopian monkeys. When the elephants were killed it is reported that the crowd expressed sympathy for them but booed Pompey, their sponsor.

The slaughter continued, as successive emperors searched for ever more exotic animals and the animal fighters dispatched them in ever more extravagant ways. Scaurus, who built an amphitheatre in Rome during the reign of Augustus, imported hippopotamuses, crocodiles and leopards. Augustus himself, by way of an ironic tribute to the deposed Queen Cleopatra and in celebration of the annexation of Egypt, imported 26 crocodiles from North Africa and had them killed in a show at the Circus Flaminius.

Claudius once organized an animal hunt in the Circus Maximus in which 30 horsemen of the Praetorian Guard, led by their tribunes and the prefect of the guard, hunted down leopards. Thessalian cavalry also took part, 'driving wild bulls all over the arena, leaping on them when they were tired out and throwing them to the ground by the horns'.

ANIMAL HUNTERS

Roman animal fighters (*venatores*) and trainers or handlers (*bestiarii*) were recruited and professionally trained at special schools alongside the gladiators, although they were always considered to be an inferior class of combatant. They are featured on many mosaics and bas-reliefs,

This third-century AD mosaic from Smirat in Tunisia commemorates a leopard hunt organized by Magerius. The beast hunters were supplied by the Telegenii agency. At the bottom left a beast fighter on stilts called Spittara is fighting a leopard called Victor.

usually wearing a standard short tunic and armed with a lance and sometimes a shield. They normally went bareheaded and bare-legged, though there are some examples showing them wearing protective helmets, body armour and greaves. A few of them appeared in the arena naked.

Groups of hunters were formed into agencies or syndicates and their owners would hire them out to the sponsors of an animal hunt. Several of these agencies, distinguished by a name, a number and an emblem, are known from inscriptions and mosaics. One of the best known of these agencies was

This mosaic, known as the 'Masked Banquet', from El Djem in Tunisia, dates from the third century AD and shows the owners of five agencies hiring out beast fighters (*venatores*). Four of the five figures are identified by their symbols; the figure second from the left is unknown, but the others, from right to left, are the bosses of the Taurisci, Pentasii, Leontinii and Telegenii agencies.

the Telegenii, no. 3, with the emblem of a crescent moon on a pole. Others included: the Taurisci, no. 2, represented by an ivy leaf; the Leontii, no. 4, identified by a millet branch; and the Pentasii, no. 5, who adopted the emblem of a five-pointed crown. A mosaic from around AD 200–220, known as the 'Masked Banquet' and found near El Djem in Tunisia, shows five bulls lying down in the arena, each one branded with an emblem representing one of five different groups of animal fighters: an ivy leaf, a millet branch, a crescent and two types of crown, one with three points and the other with five. The Telegenii feature in another mosaic of a similar date that also comes from the region around El Djem. It is the story of a leopard hunt, sponsored by a man called Magerius, and shows the different hunters at various stages of the kill. Inscriptions tell us what each hunter was called and the animals have been given names too. Presiding over the proceedings are Magerius himself, accompanied by the divine Dionysos and Diana for protection and good luck.

The fact that some creatures appearing in animal hunts were named would suggest that they survived long enough to make regular appearances and so became favourites with the crowds just like certain gladiators. One of the leopards in the Magerius mosaic is called Victor and other sources have yielded names such as Crudelis, meaning 'merciless' and Omicida, meaning 'man-killer'.

Androcles and the Lion

One of the great attractions of an animal fight was that no one could ever predict what would happen. Even a lion might decide on occasion to run away instead of standing its ground. The animals were often teased and provoked by the handlers behind the scenes to get them charged up before they were released into the arena, and sometimes they were deliberately starved to make them more aggressive.

The legend of Androcles and the Lion that has come down to us via the Roman grammarian Aulus Gellius (AD 130-180) makes a touching anecdote. There is more than one version of this story but the following account is the most well known. Androcles was a runaway slave who had been recaptured and condemned to the beasts in the Circus Maximus. He was sent into the arena to face a lion. To everyone's surprise, this lion, instead of tearing into Androcles and polishing him off in a few minutes, seemed to recognize him and began to lick him affectionately. Augustus, who was sponsoring the games on this occasion, was so intrigued by this that he called off the execution and asked Androcles what had happened. Androcles told him that he had escaped from a cruel master whilst in North Africa and fled into the desert, where he lived in a cave. One day he met a lion who was limping, clearly in some pain. Androcles removed a large thorn from the lion's paw and animal was able to walk again. The two of them lived together and the lion became his protector, but after a while Androcles got bored and decided to return to civilization. He was picked up by some soldiers and handed back to his old master, who was now in Rome. Meanwhile, the lion had been captured and taken to Rome as well, and it was this same animal who turned up in the arena when Androcles was condemned to death. Augustus was impressed and, backed by public

Androcles and the Lion depicted in a nineteenth-century etching.

demand, granted Androcles a reprieve and a pardon. From then on the former slave would often be seen walking round the city with his friend and saviour, the lion, on a lead.

DISPOSING OF THE CARCASSES

One of the logistical problems that the people who managed an amphitheatre had to deal with was the disposal of dead animals. Thousands of bones have been recovered from the Colosseum's drains, which suggests that animals would have been dumped in the basement there. Some of them would have been fed to other animals and there is literary evidence indicating that they might also have been prepared for human consumption. There is a parallel for this in Spain, where dead bulls are butchered after a bull-fight. The meat used to be distributed charitably to hospitals and poorhouses but nowadays it ends up in the markets, where it fetches higher than normal prices.

The physician Galen describes how a large elephant was dissected after appearing in the arena. The animal's heart, which was clearly a delicacy, ended up in the imperial kitchens. Apuleius mentions bear-meat being given to the poor – the animals had been imported for hunting but had died in the heat before the event.

Suetonius records that Caligula decided that butcher's meat was too expensive and ordered the flesh of executed criminals to be fed to the animals, a policy that was considered outrageous. Allowing men to be torn to pieces by animals was acceptable but that is where it ought to stop. Cassius Dio records that Claudius once had a lion destroyed because it had got used to eating human flesh. And the Christian convert Tertullian talks of:

> ... those who dine on the flesh of wild animals from the arena, keen on the meat of boar or stag. The boar in his battle has wiped the blood off him whose blood he drew; the stag has wallowed in the blood of the gladiator. The bellies of the very bears are sought, full of raw and undigested human flesh.

This was his riposte to the accusation that Christians were guilty of cannibalism, a belief no doubt derived from a misinterpretation of the passage in the gospels: '... unless you eat of my body and drink of my blood you cannot have life in you'.

ROMAN EXECUTIONS

The Romans had a rigid class structure that was reinforced by pieces of legislation that Augustus introduced when he became emperor, and methods of execution were keyed to this. The fate of a condemned nobleman was usually beheading, which was a swift death and a relatively more dignified one than the crucifixion, hanging, burning or various methods of starvation that befell the common criminal. Capital crimes in Rome at the beginning of the imperial age were, broadly, murder, treason, robbery and arson. This is much less severe than the British penal code in the years before 1832 when it is reckoned that there were 220 different offences carrying the death penalty on the statute book.

During the Republican period Roman slave-owners had absolute right of life and death over their slaves and could dispose of them at will. An owner would often choose to execute a slave in public as an example and a deterrent, and he would hire the services of a municipal undertaker who would carry out the execution and dispose of the body afterwards. An early first century BC inscription from Pozzuoli gives an account of how these executions were to be conducted.

> If anyone wishes to have a slave – male or female – punished privately, he who wishes to have the punishment inflicted shall do as follows. If he wants to put the slave on the cross or fork, the contractor must supply the posts, chains, ropes for floggers and the floggers themselves. The person having the punishment inflicted is to pay four sesterces for each of the operatives who carry the fork and the same for the floggers and for the executioner.
>
> The magistrate shall give orders for such punishments as he exacts in his public capacity, and when orders are given, [the contractor] is to be ready to exact the punishment. He is to set up crosses and supply without charge nails, pitch, wax, tapers and anything else that is necessary for this in order to deal with the condemned man. Again if he is ordered to drag away the corpse with a hook, the work gang is to be dressed in red and ring a bell while dragging away the body.

DAMNATIO AD BESTIAS

From the second century BC a slave-owner also had the option of a form of punishment known as *damnatio ad bestias* ('condemned to the beasts'), which at least gave the offender a slim chance of survival.

The earliest recorded instance of *damnatio ad bestias* was in 167 BC when Aemilius Paullus had deserters from Rome's auxiliary forces trampled to death by elephants after his victory over the Macedonian king, Perseus. Twenty-one years later his son, Scipio Aemilius, celebrated his triumph over Carthage, which had resulted in the total destruction of the city in 146 BC, and he too ordered wild animals to be let loose on the recaptured deserters under his command. At this time such methods of execution seem to have been the punishment reserved exclusively for the military. Later the practice was extended to include common criminals.

Proof that the public enjoyed public executions can be found in the souvenir items and other artefacts that these events generated, such as a small terracotta statue from Kalaa Srira (modern Tunisia) that shows a man with his hands tied behind his back riding a bull and being mauled by a leopard. The Zliten mosaic from North Africa, which dates from the first or second century AD shows condemned men bound to stakes in small carts being attacked by beasts. Another mosaic from El Djem shows a criminal on foot, with arms bound, being pushed towards a leopard.

Emperors and the organizers of the games proved to be very resourceful in devising methods of execution purely on the basis of how entertaining they would be to the public. Crucifixion, which involves a lingering death sometimes lasting for days, was not credited as having great entertainment value as it was too slow. Burning, however, was usually very dramatic, as Tacitus (AD *c.* 56-*c.* 120) observed when he described the fate of the Christians scapegoated by Nero after the fire of AD 64:

> Some were covered with skins of wild beasts and left to be devoured by
> dogs; others were nailed to crosses; numbers were burned alive and many,
> covered over with inflammable matter, were lighted up to serve as
> torches during the night.

A variation of the 'burning torches' invention was the *pyrricharii*, a method that Plutarch and Martial both describe. The condemned prisoners had to wear costumes that had been pre-soaked in an inflammable liquid. They

then had to dance before the crowd and continue dancing until they dropped down dead after their clothing had been set on fire.

The mass execution of criminals in the arena was always greatest in time of war, because anyone involved in a revolt against Rome was considered to be guilty of a capital offence. After the fall of Jerusalem in AD 70 more than 2500 Jewish prisoners were condemned to death.

If an emperor really wanted to demonstrate his omnipotence he would heighten the dramatic effect of an execution by ordering a re-enactment of stories from Greek or Roman mythology, such as that of Prometheus, whose liver was eaten by an eagle while he was chained to a rock. Nero once ordered a prisoner to fly like Icarus and ended up covered in blood when the condemned man crash-landed in front of him. Tertullian tells of prisoners impersonating the god Attis, who was castrated, and Hercules, who burnt himself to death.

Other criminals were executed in a manner that reflected the crime. The leader of a band of brigands who had terrorized the area around Mount Etna in Sicily was sent to Rome to be executed as part of a gladiatorial show held in the Forum during the reign of Augustus. The Roman geographer Strabo (*c.* 63 BC–AD *c.* 21) witnessed his death:

> I saw him torn to pieces by wild beasts ... He was put onto a tall contraption as though on Etna. The contraption suddenly disintegrated and collapsed taking him down with it onto the fragile cages of animals set up beneath the contraption for that purpose.

This scene from the Zliten mosaic in Tripoli, which is thought to date from around the second century AD, shows an execution by wild animals (*damnatio ad bestias*). At the left, two condemned men have been tied to posts. One is being attacked by a large cat. The other is being wheeled out on a small cart to face attack by a leopard.

If *damnatio ad bestias* did not appeal as a punishment then magistrates or slave-owners could send the wrongdoers into the arena to fight each other. The philosopher Seneca, writing some 35 years before the opening of the Colosseum, condemned this practice:

> All previous fighting had been merciful by comparison. Now finesse is set aside and we have pure unadulterated murder. The combatants have no protective covering; their entire bodies are exposed to the blows. No blow falls in vain. This is what most people prefer to the regular contests, and even to those which are put on by popular request. And it is obvious why. There is no helmet, no shield to repel the blade. Why have armour? Why bother with skill? All that just delays death.
>
> In the morning men are thrown to lions and bears. At midday they are thrown to the spectators themselves. No sooner is a man killed than they shout for him to kill another, or to be killed. The final victor is kept for some other slaughter. In the end every fighter dies … 'Kill him,' they shout. 'Beat him, burn him.'

In AD 61, however, the option of *damnatio ad bestias* was restricted when Nero's *lex Petronia* prevented slave-owners from punishing their slaves in this way without a court order.

DISPOSING OF THE BODIES

The treatment of the corpses of people executed in the arena is well attested. They were invariably mutilated, the face smashed in. Bodies were collected from the arena by a man dressed as Charun, carrying a sledge-hammer and a dagger. He would beat the man's head in with his hammer, stab him and then summon the attendants, who were traditionally dressed in red and carried bells, to drag the body off with a giant hook.

What happened after the corpses were removed from the arena has provoked a great deal of debate amongst the scholars. Denying a man a proper burial was considered to be part of the punishment, so there are few clues to be had in the cemeteries or other burial grounds. When the political reformer Tiberius Gracchus and three hundred of his supporters were assassinated in 133 BC the Senate refused to allow them to be buried and had all the corpses dumped into the River Tiber. It was a common fate. This is what happened to the emperor Vitellius in AD 69 according to Tacitus:

The soldiers bound his arms behind his back, put a noose around his neck and dragged him with torn garments and half naked to the Forum. All along the Sacred Way he was greeted with mockery and abuse, his head held back by the hair, as is common with criminals ... He was tortured for a long time and then dispatched and dragged off with a hook to the Tiber.

THE CHRISTIAN MARTYRS

The Romans tended not to discriminate in their attitude towards Christians and Jews. Both groups' refusal to honour Roman gods was regarded as treason. People from other religions were often willing to pay lip service to Rome, in which case Rome was generally willing to assimilate them. It was the exclusive character of Judaism and Christianity that gave them problems. The Romans believed that their gods had to be appeased by ritual and sacrifice and if the deities were not pleased they sent disasters such as plagues and earthquakes. And those who refused to perform the right rituals were often blamed for these calamities. As Tertullian put it: 'If the Tiber floods or the Nile fails to, the cry goes up: the Christians to the lion!'

The persecution of Christians started under Domitian, though it was not systematic to begin with, and continued with the reign of Trajan (AD 98-117), who tightened up the law and decided that those who refused to pay homage to the Roman gods should face the death penalty. However, Christians were not usually rounded up to be summarily executed but were carefully questioned and given every opportunity to comply with the edict. While there is some evidence that Christians were tortured during the course of these interrogations, a Roman governor in the provinces did not have the power to sentence them if they were Roman citizens – as St Paul reminded the centurion who arrested him in Jerusalem – but had to send them to Rome to be dealt with. This policy is confirmed in a letter that Pliny the Younger (AD *c.* 61-*c.* 112) wrote to Trajan in 112. Pliny was the governor of Bithynia in northwestern Asia Minor at this time and he wanted clarification on the correct procedure for dealing with the dissidents:

For the moment, this is the line I have taken with all persons brought before me on the charge of being Christians. I have asked them in person if they are Christians, and if they admit it, I repeat the question a second and third time, with a warning of the punishment awaiting them. If they persist, I order them to be led away for execution.

In his reply Trajan tells Pliny to be tolerant:

> These people must not be hunted down; if they are brought before you
> and the charge against them is proved, they must be punished, but in the
> case of anyone who denies he is a Christian, and makes it clear that he is
> not by offering prayers to our gods, he is to be pardoned as a result of his
> repentance, however suspect his past conduct may be. Pamphlets circulated
> anonymously must play no part in any accusation. They create the worst
> sort of precedent and are quite far from keeping with the spirit of our age.

This attitude seems to have been adopted by most Roman magistrates and
is confirmed in many Christian accounts of martyrdom. The examining
magistrate normally tried to get the accused to sacrifice to the emperor and
exhibit some sign of loyalty. The *Acts of the Martyrs* record that in the
case of St Polycarp (AD *c.* 69–*c.* 155), the bishop of Smyrna (Izmir), who was
burnt to death, 'the proconsul tried to persuade him and told him to have
some compassion for his own age', and at the trial of St Justin (AD *c.* 100–165)
and his companions in Rome the prefect warns them, 'If you do not obey
you will be punished.' The traditional Christian response was that they
knew 'only one Lord, King of Kings and Emperor of all peoples' and this
was totally unacceptable to the Romans. No doubt there were many Christians who were prepared to deny their faith when brought before the
courts (as they were to do during the Reformation), but hundreds refused
and finished up in the arena with the common criminals.

Such events are recorded in Christian writings. Eusebius of Caesarea
(AD *c.* 264–*c.* 340) describes the martyrdom of Christians at Tyre where leopards, bears, wild boars and bulls were goaded with hot irons but to no avail:

> The man-eating beasts for a considerable time did not dare to touch or
> even approach the bodies of those who were dear to God but made their
> attacks on the others (beast-handlers) who presumably were provoking
> and urging them on from the outside; while the holy champions were the
> only ones they did not reach at all, though they stood naked, waving
> their hands to draw them on to themselves.

Naturally, the early Christian writers claim that this miracle was due to
divine intervention. Eusebius continues: 'Then at last, after the terrible

The martyrdom of St Ignatius in the arena, depicted in an illuminated manuscript of the Eastern Church, the *Menologium of Basil II*, from the early eleventh century.

and varied assaults of these beasts, they were butchered with the sword.'

Christian persecution continued. Decius was the first emperor to instigate it as a matter of stated policy, during his reign from AD 249 to 251. Roman citizens were obliged to swear an oath of allegiance to the emperor and this involved making a sacrifice to the gods. Among those who refused to do so during this period was Pope Fabianus, who was executed. Christians went on suffering for their faith until the reign of Constantine the Great (AD 307–337). He was the first emperor to convert. He enacted the Edict of Toleration in AD 313, giving back to the Church the property that the state had confiscated, and made Christianity the official religion in AD 324. He was baptized a few weeks before he died in AD 337 and was buried in the church he had had built in Constantinople.

St Ignatius of Antioch

The Colosseum produced its first named Christian martyr, St Ignatius, the third bishop of Antioch, some time during the reign of Trajan (AD 98–117). Ignatius was arrested and interrogated in Antioch and when he refused to recant he was 'condemned to the beasts' and shipped off to Rome. He described his long journey in a series of letters (seven of them believed to be authentic), and in one of them he contemplates the fate that awaits him:

From Syria even to Rome I fight with wild beasts, by land and sea, by night and by day, being bound amidst ten leopards, even a company of soldiers, who only grow worse when they are kindly treated.

In many places along the route Christians gathered to support him but he declared his willingness to die and asked his followers not to try and dissuade him. No account of his ordeal in the arena of the Colosseum exists but it is reported that his remains were taken back to Antioch and interred there. The relics were returned to Rome in the fifth century on the orders of the emperor Theodosius II and they were placed in the former Temple of Fortune, which by then had been converted into a Christian church. Their final resting place in Rome, where they remain today, is the church of St Clement's.

ENTER THE GLADIATORS

After the wild animal hunts and the midday executions came the *munus*, the gladiatorial show that was the highlight of the day's entertainment. Several days before an important show notices would go up around the city announcing who would be appearing and the order in which the fights were due to take place. League tables were distributed so that people could bet on the outcome of the fights based on a gladiator's past record. There were programmes and scorecards so that you could keep track of the contests – V for a victory, M (*missus*) for a gladiator who had been defeated but not killed and θ (*theta*) for a gladiator who had been killed.

There are examples of some of these announcements, which were painted in red on the walls of houses at Pompeii:

Thirty pairs of gladiators furnished by Gnaeus Alleius Nigidius Maius, the quinquennial *duumvir*, together with their substitutes, will fight at Pompeii on 24, 25 and 26 November. There will be a hunt. Hurrah for Maius the quinquennial! Bravo Paris.

Another dated to the time of Claudius reads:

Twenty pairs of gladiators furnished by Decimus Lucretius Satrius Valens, permanent priest of Nero, son of the emperor, and ten pairs of gladiators furnished by Decimus Lucretius Valens, his son, will fight at Pompeii on 8, 9, 10, 11 and 12 April. There will be a big hunt, and awnings.

The advertisements in Rome always contained the claim '... *quos nec spectasset quisquam nec spectaturus esset*' ('... which no one has ever seen or would ever see again').

Plutarch records that on the eve of the games the gladiators would be given a good meal and put on show for anyone who wanted to view them. Like punters looking at the horses before a race, people would study form and pick out their favourites before deciding how to place their bets. On the morning of the *munus* the gladiators would gather at their barracks and stay there while the animal hunts were taking place. They would then march in a solemn procession (*pompa*) to the amphitheatre together with the organizers of the games, their *lanistas*, the referees, and other

Painting after a funerary relief from Pompeii showing the procession (*pompa*) that began the gladiatorial games.

arena personnel such as stretcher-bearers and armourers. The procession would also include all the condemned criminals. The procession was always led by the magistrate who was sponsoring the games, accompanied by his lictors carrying bundles of rods and axes (the symbols of the magistrate's power to whip and execute) marching ahead of him. If he were a praetor he would be accompanied by six lictors whereas a consul had twelve.

There is an illustration of a gladiatorial procession on a bas-relief from a tomb at Pompeii, now in the collection of the Naples Museum. (A painting of the relief is shown on pages 126-7.) It shows two lictors dressed in togas, carrying rods and axes. They are followed by three cloaked figures blowing long trumpets. Behind the trumpeters there are four men in tunics carrying a bier on their shoulders with two small figures (possibly armourers) on top, one wielding a hammer. Behind the bier are two more men in tunics carrying placards, probably proclaiming the crimes the condemned men had committed, the names of the gladiators due to fight, and the order of play so to speak. Next comes a man in a toga, presumably the magistrate who is hosting the games (known as the *editor*). Following him there are six men carrying helmets and shields. They are probably armour-bearers because gladiators would have been wearing purple cloaks embroidered in gold. The first two men carry small round shields, identifying them as possibly coming from the Thracian camp. Then there are two men blowing horns (*cornua*). Several of these instruments were found in the gladiator barracks at Pompeii. Right at the end of the procession are two horsemen, who would probably have opened the show with a demonstration of mounted combat. This example is a wonderful record but should be accepted as an artistic interpretation of what a gladiatorial procession would have involved. Even in Pompeii a *munus* would have involved more than three pairs of gladiators and in Rome, especially at the Colosseum, there would have been many more.

THE WARM-UP

A *munus* always kicked off with a few warm-up acts to get the spectators in the mood for the gladiatorial contests to follow. These took the form of freak shows with dwarfs and cripples, mock fights, men on stilts goading animals, displays on horseback, performances by acrobats and jugglers,

theatrical scenes, masquerades and tableaux. All of this went on against a background of loud music.

The Roman philosopher and orator Apuleius (b. *c.* AD 123) describes one of these acts in his satirical novel *The Golden Ass*. Three young women playing the parts of the goddesses Minerva, Juno and Venus re-enact the 'Judgement of Paris'. Venus, the goddess of love, is attended by a number of plump little boys dressed as cupids and a troupe of girls representing the graces and seasons, who dance and lay flowers in her path. The goddess is unclothed 'to show her perfect beauty; all naked save that her fine and comely middle was lightly covered with a thin silken smock, and this the wanton wind blew hither and thither ...' and Mercury, the messenger of the gods, played by a handsome youth, is also naked, except for his winged hat and sandals. Paris, the abductor of Helen of Troy, is tending goats on a hill. When he declares Venus to be the most beautiful of the three goddesses, Minerva and Juno leave, vowing vengeance on him, while Venus and her entourage dance triumphantly around the arena. A stream running down the hill turns red, presaging the bloodletting of the Trojan War.

This scene from the Zliten mosaic shows a band of musicians: a trumpeter, a woman playing the water organ and two horn players. The curious bed-like object in the background is probably a stretcher with a pillow at the far end.

THE MAIN ATTRACTION

When the warm-up was over the gladiatorial procession entered the arena by the ceremonial entrance at the western end of the long axis and halted in front of the imperial box where all the participants saluted the emperor. There followed the ritual testing of weapons and the preparation of punishments for any gladiators who did not fight properly: the whip, cane and heated iron bar. At this point the *tiros* had to endure an initiation ceremony in which they were whipped by officials dressed up as demons. The *equites* cantered round the arena while the gladiators prepared. The trumpets sounded, the gladiators moved to the edge of the arena and the horsemen charged. When the cavalry battle was finished the trumpets sounded again and the gladiators took the stage. Some scholars argue that several pairs of gladiators fought in the arena at the same time but others claim that there is no real proof of this. The only clue is that several visual representations appear to show more than one fight taking place in the arena, but as pictures cannot truly show the passage of time they cannot be accepted as conclusive. It would certainly have made the task of the referees more difficult if they had to keep track of more than one contest at a time, and would certainly have been a problem for the emperor when it came to his final decision on the outcome of a fight.

THE KILL

A gladiator might well be killed by a blow inflicted during the fight but more often one of the gladiators would be overcome by his opponent, probably badly wounded. If he felt unable to go on he would signal his submission to the referee by holding up his left index finger or fall to his knees and let his shield drop. In the latter case he would reverse his sword, holding it by the tip. The trumpets would sound the submission. The victorious gladiator was forbidden by law to go in for the kill. Originally, because of the sacrificial character of the fights, the fallen gladiator would automatically have been killed. This had become less common during the late Republic but some sadistic *editors* such as Nero's grandfather, Ahenobarbus, insisted on their 'pound of flesh'. Augustus strongly disapproved of this and tried to persuade Ahenobarbus to be more moderate but when he persisted the emperor passed a law putting an end to this savage practice.

When the losing gladiator held up his finger asking for mercy the referee would intervene. Several pictures show him holding back the victorious gladiator. The referee would look to the *editor* for his decision while the crowd yelled their opinion. If the fallen gladiator had fought well they would shout '*missus*' calling for his life to be spared. If he had fought badly they would shout '*verbera*' (whip), '*ure*' (burn) or '*iugula*' (kill), and signal their displeasure with their thumbs (*pollice verso*). The *editor* would signal his decision to the referee, usually following the wishes of the crowd but not always. There was always an outside chance of a reprieve, as Juvenal

This fragment of bas-relief held at the Glyptothek museum in Munich shows the end of a gladiatorial contest. The hand emerging from behind the trumpeter's tunic, with its index finger and forefinger extended, may provide evidence of what the *missus* gesture (the signal indicating that a gladiator's life should be spared) looked like.

observed: 'Even a gladiator who has been defeated in the savage arena continues to hope although the crowd threatens him with hostile thumb.'

The *pollice verso* gesture does not necessarily mean the same as a modern 'thumbs down' sign and there is no evidence whatsoever for the Romans using a 'thumbs up' gesture to indicate that they wanted the life of a fallen gladiator to be spared. A fragment of a bas-relief held by the Glyptothek museum in Munich shows two gladiators, one sitting on the ground and the other standing above him, sword raised waiting for the order to kill or spare. Opposite are several trumpeters sounding the end of the contest. Extending from behind these trumpeters is a hand with its index finger and forefinger extended. It would be difficult to interpret this as anything other than the sign for sparing the life of the fallen gladiator. This being so, the *pollice verso* could just as well mean 'thumbs up' or more likely 'thumbs forward', imitating a sword thrust.

If the verdict was for death, the defeated gladiator would extend his neck and the victor would thrust his sword into the man's throat, dispatching him quickly and cleanly. The code of the gladiators was all about dying well and his comrades would make sure that the *coup de grâce* was delivered as painlessly as possible. There are many mosaics, graffiti and sculptures depicting this moment.

AFTER THE FIGHT

After the fight the emperor would present the victorious gladiator with a palm branch and, if his performance had been particularly good, a crown. Like modern sporting heroes the triumphant winner would then do a lap of honour around the arena, waving the tokens of his victory to the crowd. It is uncertain whether successful gladiators and those who had been spared left the arena by the ceremonial entrance or by the death gate.

Winners also received prize money according to a scale stipulated in the gladiators' contract. Marcus Aurelius regulated this prize money, relating it to the purchase price of the individual gladiator. The maximum reward was set at one fifth of his purchase price for a slave and a quarter for a freeman. The crowd enjoyed joining in with this part of the ceremony, counting out loud as the *editor* handed out the gold coins to the winner.

We cannot be certain exactly how a gladiator's body was treated after death. Tertullian implies that all the corpses were abused and desecrated, whether they were Christian martyrs, common criminals or brave gladiators:

> We have laughed, amid the noon's blend of cruelty and absurdity, at Mercury using his burning iron to see who was dead. We have seen Jupiter's brother [Pluto], too, conducting out the corpses of gladiators, hammer in hand.

Maybe Tertullian was confused here. Gladiatorial contests were held in the afternoons whereas noon was the time when the Christians were executed or thrown to the beasts alongside the criminals. They suffered the same fate because the Romans viewed both groups as lawbreakers who were therefore equally culpable.

From other sources it is possible to draw a reasonably accurate picture of what actually happened after the games. When a gladiator died after combat two officials and a pair of stretcher-bearers would enter the arena. One official was dressed as Mercury and he carried a caduceus in the form of a red-hot wand. The second official was dressed and armed as Charun. Mercury would touch the body with his wand to make sure that the gladiator really was dead. If not, then Charun would cut his throat. The stretcher-bearers would then lift the body onto a stretcher and exit through the Gate of the Dead. One of these stretchers, shown on the Zliten mosaic from Libya (see page 129), is more like a bed than the accepted notion of a stretcher. It even has a cushion at one end for the wounded gladiator to rest his head. It has been suggested that these stretchers doubled up as operating tables and that one of the rooms flanking the gladiators' entrance to the arena could have been used as an operating theatre.

The evidence from the posters advertising gladiatorial contests at Pompeii implies that the mortality rates for gladiators was not all that high. Popular gladiators who had survived four or five matches could rely on the crowd to save their lives if they lost. These posters refer to men who had survived 20 or even 30 fights but had only won about half of them. Clearly if you put on a good show you were unlikely to be killed. But this was not always the case. The sadistic emperor Caracalla developed a particular dislike for a gladiator named Bato and refused to let him leave the arena after he had won his fight, forcing him to face a second opponent. When Bato won this fight as well, the emperor forced him to fight a third contest, which he lost. Caracalla refused to reprieve him and so he was killed by his final opponent.

THE OPENING OF THE COLOSSEUM

Cassius Dio tells us that the official opening of the Colosseum in AD 80 was marked with events held at several different venues all over the city and the celebrations lasted for a hundred days. On the opening day gladiatorial contests followed by beast hunts were held at Augustus's Old Naumachia in the Campus Martius, which been boarded over to create an arena. On the second day there were horse races, presumably in the Circus Maximus. This gave the organizers time to remove the boards and flood the *naumachia* so that a sea-battle could be held there on the third day. This battle, involving three thousand men, was a fanciful re-enactment of the Siege of Syracuse by the Athenians, who made a seaborne landing on the island of Ortyga and captured the town wall in the fifth century.

We unfortunately have very little information about the events that took place at the Colosseum during this time and Cassius Dio gives only a brief account:

> There was a battle between cranes and also between four elephants;
> animals both tame and wild were slain to the number of nine thousand
> and women (not those of any prominence, however) took part in
> despatching them. As for the men, several fought in single combat and
> several groups contended together in infantry and naval battles.

In Martial's description of the opening ceremony at the Colosseum in AD 80 he says that the games began with an event that was entirely political: the public humiliation and banishment of informers. This was something that Titus had vowed to do when he first became emperor. Suetonius says that the traitors were first scourged in the Forum and then paraded in the Amphitheatre. Some were sold into slavery and the others banished.

There followed a number of warm-up events, including a re-enactment of the Greek myth of Europa, carried off by Jupiter in the guise of a white bull: 'The bull was snatched up in the midst of the arena and departed for the stars.' This recalls the effects known as *deus ex machina*, commonly used in Greek theatres, when the gods appeared and disappeared – as if by magic but in fact thanks to a backstage system of mechanical cranes. There were other less savoury allusions to mythology. Martial's apparently innocuous couplet says it all: 'Believe that Pasiphae was mated by the

Dictaean bull; we have seen it, the old legend has won credence.' According to the legend, Pasiphae, wife of Minos, the king of Crete, fell in love with a bull and had a full-size model of a cow made so that she could lie inside it and encourage the bull to mate with her. The product of this union was the monstrous Minotaur – half man, half bull. Nero had staged something similar and claimed that a bull had mated with a woman concealed in a wooden model of a cow. Suetonius says that many believed this but how it had been achieved in the arena is difficult to imagine.

Martial gives a wealth of detail about the animal fights that appear to have been held on the opening day. His list of all the animals that were hunted and killed in the arena includes lions, leopards, tigers, wild boar and bears. He and Cassio Dio both claim that some of the animals, particularly lions, were killed by women, perhaps in the guise of Diana the Huntress. A touch of black comedy was added when a pregnant sow was

Detail from the Piazza Armerina mosaic showing men dragging a bull.

speared and gave birth to a piglet. Many of the contests involved animals fighting animals. Martial describes how the crowd grew restless when one of the animals got bored and refused to fight:

> While trembling trainers were goading the rhinoceros and the great
> beast's anger was long agathering ... but at length the fury we earlier
> knew returned. For with his double horn he tossed a heavy bear as a
> bull tosses dummies.

A terracotta relief from Rome showing *venatores* fighting lions and bears.

It is not known for certain how many animals were killed, either on the opening day of the games or during the three-month-long inaugural celebrations, but because it was such a high-profile event it is bound to have

been a very large number. Estimates range from Dio's nine thousand in total to Suetonius's astounding five thousand a day.

Executions were usually reserved for the midday break, but Martial's account of the games in AD 80 implies that were integrated into the animal fights for he describes two men being savaged by bears, then a man being crucified and having his stomach torn out by a Caledonian bear, followed by women hunting lions and then a fight between a rhinoceros and a bull. Such executions were often dressed up as mythological scenes. Martial describes one such condemned man dressed as Orpheus charming the animals which lay down beside him. Perhaps the poor wretch did not know what was going to happen but suddenly a trapdoor opened and a disenchanted bear with no ear for music wandered over and tore him to pieces. No doubt this appealed to the Roman sense of humour.

Most of Martial's description of the gladiatorial events has been lost, and Cassio Dio tells us very little about the gladiatorial fights that followed the opening ceremony at the Colosseum. Dio refers to individual combats and battles. An isolated verse in Martial tells of two gladiators, Priscus and Verus, who fought with such skill and bravery that the long-drawn-out contest failed to produce a victor. With the approval of the crowd Titus awarded the accoutrements of victory – the palm and crown – to both men.

THE NAUMACHIA

The name given to an aquatic display in Roman times was *naumachia* and the word applied both to the event and the venue where it took place. These displays were usually presented in the form of re-enactments, either legendary or historical, and to begin with they were held on lakes or man-made pools. The question of whether *naumachiae* were ever held at the Colosseum is one that has exercised historians and archaeologists for centuries. If the Amphitheatre was *not* designed to be flooded, why was it built on marshland when other, more suitable sites were available?

Opposite
This German painting of 1817 depicts a *naumachia* in an amphitheatre.

The mock naval battles that the Romans flocked to see were like the gladiatorial shows in one major respect: most of the men taking part were slaves, condemned criminals or prisoners of war, and many of them would end up being killed in front of the crowds. Aquatic spectacles usually entailed the re-enactment of a legendary or actual sea-battle. Whether the spectators knew their history or not was irrelevant, as the reason for choosing a particular battle lay in its dramatic potential. Cassius Dio describes one battle, between the Corinthians and the Corcyrians (the ancient inhabitants of Corfu), where the object was to capture an island that had been re-created in the middle of the arena. The ever-popular Siege of Syracuse and the Battle of Salamis were often chosen for the same reason.

EARLY AQUATIC DISPLAYS

The *naumachia* that Julius Caesar put on in Rome as part of his triumph in 46 BC is the first one ever recorded. He had a pool excavated in the Campus Martius, and galleys with two, three and four banks of oars powered by three thousand oarsmen re-enacted a sea-battle between the Phoenicians and Egyptians. The pool remained for several years after Caesar's death but there is no record of any other shows being held there. When the area suffered an outbreak of the plague, stagnant water was declared to be the source and the pool was filled in.

Augustus staged a similar event in 2 BC to celebrate the inauguration of his newly built Temple of Mars the Avenger. He had a huge basin excavated on the site of Caesar's villa beside the Tiber that measured 536×357 metres and then flooded it. The historic event that he chose to re-enact was the naval battle where the Persian king Xerxes was defeated by the Athenians in 480 BC, and there was an area of land in the middle of the pond that represented the island of Salamis where the engagement had occurred. It is reported that six thousand men were involved in the battle altogether. This venue became a permanent site for sea-battles and was later referred to as the Old Naumachia.

It is not surprising that once Augustus had staged his first aquatic shows most of the emperors who followed him added the *naumachia* to their list of entertainments intended to win popularity with the citizens

This photograph taken in the late nineteenth century shows the basement of the Colosseum flooded.

of Rome. Tacitus tells us that Claudius staged the most remarkable of these aquatic displays on the Fucine Lake, 80 kilometres east of Rome, in AD 52 to celebrate the building of a tunnel through the mountains joining the lake to the River Liris. Claudius gave the command for a hundred galleys with two and three banks of oars to be launched, manned by 19,000 men – convicted criminals dressed as naval personnel from the warring island of Rhodes and Sicily. The area reserved for the battle was surrounded with a line of rafts to stop any of them escaping. Cohorts of the Praetorian Guard armed with catapults and protected with palisades were placed on the rafts and the lake was also patrolled by ships filled with marines. The spectators sat on the surrounding hills. Suetonius described the show, observing that the men shouted the customary salute to the emperor: *'Morituri te salutant'* ('They who are about to die salute you') to which Claudius replied '*Aut non*' ('Or not'). Believing that they had just been pardoned, the men decided they did not need to fight. Claudius leapt from his throne and ran along the edge of the lake 'with his ridiculous tottering gait' issuing both threats and inducements until they finally agreed to start the battle. The signal to commence was sounded on a trumpet by a man dressed in silver to represent the sea-god Triton, who was brought up into the centre of the lake on a mechanically operated platform.

When the display was over and Claudius had kept his promise not to execute the prisoners who had taken part, the engineers began to drain the lake. At this late stage they discovered that the tunnel had been excavated at the wrong level and it needed to be deeper. A new tunnel was built and Claudius arranged another public display, this time a contest in which two armies of gladiators were put to battle on pontoons built over the lake. He held a banquet for his guests on the shores of the lake near the entrance to the tunnel, but when the sluices were opened to drain the lake the rush of the water was so fierce that the banks collapsed and everything in its path was washed away.

Nero loved organizing naval battles and Suetonius and Cassius Dio both record that he had salt water brought in specially for one of his extravaganzas. Like Julius Caesar before him he chose to re-enact the Battle of Salamis but went one better by introducing sea monsters into the scenario as well. Some of his events appear to have been staged on his famous *stagnum*, the ornamental lake in the grounds of his Golden Palace.

When Titus used Augustus's Old Naumachia for a show, it is reported that he had the arena covered with planks resting on piles so that he could stage a gladiatorial contest and an animal hunt on the first day and a chariot race on the second day. On the third day the flooring was removed for a sea-battle between three thousand Syracusans and Athenians. During the battle the Athenians landed on an island and captured a fort there.

Domitian created another arena for sea-battles beyond the Tiber, near the Vatican Hill, which became known as the New Naumachia. Cassius Dio describes one show that was held there where practically all the contestants and many of the spectators died in a violent storm that suddenly broke out. Domitian apparently refused to allow anyone to leave or take cover. According to Martial, Domitian's displays in the New Naumachia were superior to all others.

THE *NAUMACHIA* CONTROVERSY

When Vespasian first conceived of the idea of an all-purpose amphitheatre on the site of Nero's Golden Palace he probably wanted to turn the lake into a *naumachia*. By choosing this spot he thought he had solved the problem of water supply because the lake was situated on natural marshland fed by the Labican Stream and other minor watercourses flowing down from the surrounding hills. But while the site seemed ideal for the purpose, the unstable ground created far greater problems when it came to building the spectator areas.

Vespasian's ambition was never realized in his lifetime, and while Titus carried on where his father had left off there is no conclusive evidence of a *naumachia* at the Colosseum at the time of the inauguration of the building in AD 80. Although a massive six-metre deep pit existed beneath the area, it would have required some method by which the 76-metre long by 44-metre wide basement could have been flooded for a sea-battle and then drained and boarded over for the next gladiatorial contest. And while there is plentiful

The fan-shaped area at the eastern end of the basement may have been used for housing galleys for the *naumachia*.

archaeological evidence to show how the arena was boarded over in Titus's time, there is no trace of any mechanism for flooding it. (The underground systems at the Colosseum are described in further detail in Appendix I.)

The possibility of a *naumachia* at the Colosseum is a controversy that has divided the experts for centuries, often with a great deal of acrimony, but there is no simple answer to the question: could naval battles ever have been staged there? The only possible reply to the question is: yes, possibly, but ... That is the answer now and almost certainly it always will be the answer. On the face of it, the proposition is absurd, yet the Romans themselves seem to have believed it. Many fantastic theories have been put forward. When John Henry Parker, curator of the Ashmolean Museum in Oxford, gave his account of the excavations in the basement at the Colosseum in 1874–75 he suggested that boats would have floated down either side of the central corridor, firing missiles at each other. There are other even more ludicrous theories. All have quite rightly been dismissed with contempt.

The attitude of scholars now towards the possibility of there ever having been a *naumachia* at the Colosseum ranges from the enthusiastic advocate through the possible believer to the agnostic and on to the sceptical analyst and the downright, adamant refusenik. Even so, there is one question that has never been satisfactorily answered: if Vespasian did not intend to hold aquatic events in his amphitheatre why did he choose to build it on the site of Nero's Pond? He was a renowned skinflint and it seems unlikely that he would have wasted money draining a lake unnecessarily.

It is now generally accepted that there was a time lapse of at least a few years between the completion of the perimeter wall of the basement with all its fittings and the building of the mural structures in the basement, during which time it could have been be used as a pool. A survey of the southwestern sector of the basement published in 1991 showed that much of the perimeter wall had been waterproofed.

The monumental survey of the basement that the German architect Heinz-Jurgen Beste carried out in the late 1990s showed there is evidence for the *naumachia* and he even refers to Titus's era as the 'naumachia period'. However, he also concluded there was no way the area could be flooded quickly or easily. This is the position that many scholars now adopt.

The only way to introduce a large quantity of water into the Colosseum basement quickly would have been through the building's very substantial drainage conduits. An examination of the north and south drainage conduits during the 1970s, together with the basement floor itself, showed that everything sloped outwards and was clearly designed for drainage. Furthermore, the conduits do not appear to connect up with a water source and such a system would wash back the sewage. However, the Italian engineer Leonardo Lombardi, in his substantial article on water supply and drainage in the Colosseum (published in English in 2001), admits that when the water in the Tiber was high it would cause a back-flow up the drainage system and flood the basement. This proves that it was not impossible but would require the use of sluice gates. The operation of such a back-flow system would require large cisterns on the higher ground around the Amphitheatre. The back-flow of the sewage is the biggest problem.

The current theory that it could be done with the water entering the Colosseum for the latrines and drinking fountains, by utilizing the rain drainage channels to deliver it to the basement, is far too complicated. Though ingenious, moving the water in this way would be far too ineffi-cient and slow. Domitian may indeed have used this method later but, to create the effect described by Martial, it must have been possible to do it in a quicker and simpler way.

Titus probably wanted to stage the series of sea-battles his father had planned for the Colosseum but no water supply system was in place in time for the opening. The original intention was probably to build under-ground aqueducts to channel the water to the Amphitheatre where they would connect up with the huge outflow conduits beneath the four tunnels. It is possible that because the builders had run out of time they could have gone for a makeshift solution of installing temporary wood-lined conduits to channel water from sources on higher ground. These would have connected up with the main drainage conduits at the point at which they emerged from the basement, causing minimum back-flow of sewage. The short section under the building itself could have been cleaned out during the night before the event. It must be pointed out that this could not be done after the drainage system was completed. Whilst there is no direct evidence to support this theory there is abundant evidence that the drainage system was incomplete at the time of the opening. The south and west radial conduits were both altered at the time of Domitian; the brick drain connecting with the western main axis conduit was not even built before then and there are signs of alterations within the conduit itself showing a change of function. It is known that at some point after the death of Titus Domitian decided to abandon the *naumachia* project altogether. His conversion of the basement with repairs is in virtually the same state as it is today. (The details of this hypothesis can be found in Appendix I.)

During aquatic shows the lifts in the vaulted chambers along the perimeter wall would be hoisted up behind the grilles so that small boats could shelter unseen under them and then shoot out suddenly to thrill the audience. A shaft just under 0.5 metres wide was inserted behind the back wall of each of the chambers. It had an outlet halfway down the wall. These may initially have housed a counterweight for the lift. Later they became a rainwater conduit. The modern theory proposes that it was these shafts that were utilized when the arena was flooded, but they were clearly never designed for this purpose.

THE OPENING OF THE COLOSSEUM

There are three main literary sources indicating that Titus held a *naumachia* when the Colosseum was inaugurated in AD 80 – the accounts left by Martial, Cassius Dio and Suetonius. All of them say something about the aquatic displays that took place but none of them really tells us all that much. Nor do they place the events specifically in the Colosseum. Martial's references merely imply a sea-battle and the appearance of sea monsters and he deals with the whole thing in just four verses.

First of all he talks of the miraculous change from the terrestrial to the aquatic and back again:

Opposite
Titus, the son of Vespasian, inaugurated the Colosseum in AD 80 following his father's death. Although he is known to have held *naumachiae* around this time, there is no direct evidence that any of these took place in the Colosseum.

> If you are here from a distant land, a late spectator for whom this was the first day of the sacred show, let not the naval warfare deceive you with its ships, and the water like to a sea: here but lately was land. You don't believe it? Watch while the waters weary Mars. But a short time hence you will be saying: 'Here but lately was sea.'

He then describes the tragic tale of Leander, swimming backwards and forwards across the Hellespont to visit his lover, Hero the priestess, until

for the next event; no doubt the authorities had devised some excruciating but entertaining executions involving the use of water.

During the night the waters would have to be drained and the floor of the arena relaid. This would require thousands of wooden parts, piles, beams, trapdoors, floorboards and wooden pegs. Sections of the floor containing trapdoors would have been prefabricated, with all parts earmarked for specific locations given a number and divided into sets. It must have been a mad rush to get it all done in time.

AFTER TITUS

According to Suetonius, Domitian held at least one aquatic show in the Colosseum. However, it is clear that at some time Domitian decided to abandon the Colosseum *naumachia* and construct a permanent arena, though it is a decision that has gone unrecorded in any of the ancient sources. Perhaps the operation of aquatic displays in the Amphitheatre was too complicated or, more likely, the wooden floors and the piles supporting them were showing signs of weakening and beginning to rot. There may have been other reasons. Suetonius mentions 'a new *naumachia*', which is confirmed by Cassius Dio. The impetus for Domitian's change of direction was probably his plans to build the new Flavian Palace on the Palatine Hill. Begun in AD 81 and completed about eleven years later, it involved the diversion of the Claudian aqueduct to supply it with water.

THE FALL OF THE COLOSSEUM

'From the great multitude of wondrous things, I would select the Colosseum as the object that affected me the most. It is stupendous, yet beautiful in its destruction.... To walk beneath its crumbling walls, to climb its shattered steps, to wander through its long, arched passages, to tread in the footsteps of Rome's ancient kings, to muse upon its broken height, is to lapse into sad, though not unpleasing, meditation.... It was once the crater of human passions; there their terrible fires blazed forth with desolating power.... But now all is still desolation.'

Thomas Cole, American landscape painter, *Notes at Naples* (1832)

Opposite
The Colosseum in Rome (detail) by the English artist J. M. W. Turner (1775–1851).

The popularity of the games continued for as long as Rome retained its empire. Trajan, returning from the conquest of Dacia (modern Romania), early in the second century AD, brought back 10,000 prisoners and 11,000 wild beasts to fight in the arena. His successor, Hadrian, sponsored six consecutive days of gladiatorial bouts and, according to the *Historia Augusta* (a somewhat unreliable source), took part in some of the fights himself. Antoninus Pius, who succeeded Hadrian, is said to have introduced the first hyena into the arena.

There was a serious fire during Antoninus Pius's reign (AD 138–161) that caused considerable damage to the Colosseum. The building was particularly vulnerable to fire because of the amount of wood used for the flooring and the uppermost seating area; a lot of the machinery, scenery and other props situated beneath the arena would have been made of wood, too. Because of its shape the *cavea* would have acted as a funnel, drawing the flames upwards to consume the wooden seats at the highest level. And although the marble and travertine would have survived the flames, the intense heat would have calcined it, causing it to split.

The philosopher emperor Marcus Aurelius was no lover of the Colosseum but he paid lip service to tradition by putting on shows and turning up in person from time to time. If by doing this he was seeking to avoid public discontent, he only partly succeeded, for he often offended the crowd by reading, writing letters and entertaining his friends in the royal box instead of paying attention to the fights.

The third century AD was a disastrous time for Rome. Successive military dictatorships created instability and to many it seemed that the empire would disintegrate. The Colosseum itself almost seemed to echo the groans of the empire. On 23 August AD 217 it went up in flames again, this time after a lightning strike. Cassius Dio reported the event:

> The hunting theatre was struck by thunderbolts on the very day of the *Vulcanalia*, and such a blaze followed that its entire upper circuit and everything in the arena was consumed, and thereupon the rest of the structure was ravaged by the flames and reduced to ruins. Neither human aid could avail against the conflagration although practically every aqueduct was emptied – nor could the downpour from the sky which was most heavy and violent, accomplish anything – to such an extent was the water from both sources consumed by the power of the thunderbolts.

In the early third century AD, 60 lift shafts were installed in the passage-ways on either side of the central corridor of the arena basement. The housings for the pulleys, made of re-used travertine, are still clearly visible.

The rebuilding of the Colosseum took more than two decades, though the work was sufficiently advanced for a rededication ceremony to be held in AD 222. Until then the games were transferred to the Circus Maximus.

The archaeologist Lynne Lancaster surveyed the site in the 1990s and identified the different building techniques used for the repairs, showing that the whole of the northwest sector of the building had suffered massive damage during the fire. The outer part of the *cavea* from entrances

40 to 47 had to be totally rebuilt from the ground up. The damage was more serious in the upper levels and more than a quarter of the total circuit needed to be reconstructed, including the area above the magistrates' entrance. In the area of the ceremonial entrance of the gladiators at the west end, the fire damage extended right down into the basement. This section had to be almost totally rebuilt.

The area beneath the arena had also suffered badly and the walls had collapsed in many places. In order to strengthen the brick supporting arches constructed in the time of Trajan, secondary arches were built inside them. The lower part of some of the tufa walls were encased in brick, and low brick arches were built across some of the corridors to support the walls. At some time within the next half century the function of the central corridor was modified. The massive trapdoors originally used to raise the expanding scenery were either reduced in width or abandoned altogether. Sixty new lift shafts, operated by a counterweight system, were inserted into the passageways on either side of the central corridor. The housings for the pulleys were made of reused travertine. These lift shafts, measuring approximately 0.9 × 1.7 metres, are somewhat smaller than those installed in the time of Domitian and could hardly have transported anything larger than a medium-sized cat. A further 36 even smaller lifts were established in the two D-shaped areas.

The archways of the Colosseum and other similar entertainment venues became a favourite haunt for prostitutes. The emperor Alexander Severus (AD 222-235) fittingly earmarked taxes paid by prostitutes for the rebuilding of the Amphitheatre. It is worth noting that the word fornication is derived from the Latin word *fornices* meaning 'arches'.

Gordian I, during his one-year reign in AD 238, modified the entertainment calendar to provide one show every month. The rather unreliable sources for this period claim that he supplied between 150 and 500 gladiators for each show. He also exhibited a hundred lions on one day and a thousand bears on another.

The great earthquake of 262 must have taken its toll, but the Colosseum was in use again when Aurelian held his great games in 274. Salvation for Rome came ten years later when Diocletian was declared emperor by his troops. His accession at last brought stable government back to the empire. Diocletian was just the strong man Rome needed at the time. His rule is universally admired by historians, but in the latter part of his reign his love for the old Roman traditions led to the last great persecu-tion of the Christians who had lived in reasonable security since the rescript of Gallienus in 260 granting an amnesty to Christians after the few years of repression initiated by his father. The Colosseum was struck by lightning again in 320 but this time there was little damage.

The accession of Constantine the Great in 307 and the acceptance of Christianity as the official religion of Rome brought about some reform but not perhaps as much as might have been expected. The Church's con-tinuing opposition to gladiatorial shows is well documented. Tertullian, who was particularly outspoken on the subject, called the Colosseum 'a temple consecrated to demons'. Bowing eventually to pressure from the Christians, Constantine stopped the courts from sending criminals to the gladiator schools – he allowed them to be sentenced to hard labour in the mines instead. His position on this matter was anomalous for, although he had cut off one of the prime sources of recruitment to the schools, gladia-torial contests were not forbidden. An inscription found in 1733 near the amphitheatre at Spello records Constantine giving permission for the Umbrians to hold gladiatorial contests in the 330s.

Emperor Constantine's decision to move the capital of the Roman Empire to Constantinople in AD 330 marked the beginning of the end for the Colosseum.

Constantine's decision in AD 330 to move the capital of the Roman Empire to Constantinople marked the beginning of the decline of Rome, and the importance of the Colosseum declined with it. Constantius II, visiting Rome in 357, inspected the *cavea*, which, according to the *Ammianus Marcellinus*, was still in excellent condition. The games continued throughout the fourth century AD despite the occasional ban. Valentinian I's edict of 365 expressly forbade sentencing Christians to the arena. But gladiato-rial shows continued, as is shown by the legislation of the late fourth-century emperors Arcadius and Hono-rius, both of whom prohibited senators from using gladiators as private bodyguards. This legislation threat-ened offending gladiators with exile and it is the last surviving legislative act relating to them. It is known from a letter that the orator Quintus Aurelius Sym-machus wrote that he donated large sums of money to help his son put on gladiatorial games at Constantinople in 393. This letter is particularly interesting as the orator

Opposite
A view of the southern side of the Colosseum from which materials were systematically quarried for centuries. The outer circuit corridors have now completely disappeared from this section. The Arch of Constantine can be seen at the bottom left of this picture.

had prevailed upon Emperor Honorius to give him 29 Saxon prisoners to kill in the arena, but the men committed suicide rather than take part in the spectacle. The letter also confirms that there were still free men willing to serve as gladiators and Symmachus praises their dedication to the sport.

The long-drawn-out death pangs of Rome began when the city was besieged by the Goths under Alaric in 408 and finally sacked in 410. During the two-year siege the dead had to be buried within the city walls and cemeteries dating from this time were discovered on the northeast side of the Colosseum piazza in 1895. After the retreat of the Goths these burial grounds were reclaimed and the graves covered with 2 metres of earth.

The Colosseum was damaged during the siege and was deserted for several years afterwards. The traumatic effect of the sacking of the Eternal City caused as much as half the population to abandon the city. Valentinian III attempted to repopulate it a generation or so later but further invasions just caused more people to migrate. The Colosseum was restored between 417 and 423 but it was damaged again by two more earthquakes, one in 429 and another in 443. The highest level of seating collapsed and the debris crashed through the arena floor into the basement. At some stage the drains were also damaged on the south side of the building and the basement was flooded. Once again the building was repaired in places but not restored entirely. By the time the last Western Roman emperor, Romulus Augustulus, was deposed in 476 the population of Rome was estimated to have been as low as 100,000.

By this time the despoliation of the Colosseum had already begun. Archaeological investigation has shown that even before the end of the fourth century the building was being robbed. Lead pipes were stripped out and some of the latrines and fountains ceased to function. By the middle of the fifth century the stonework was at risk. An inscription found in the Colosseum records that the senator Gerontius was given permission to 'quarry' by Theodosius, indicating that the vandalism was officially sanctioned.

Gladiatorial shows had been officially abolished by Valentinian III in 438, although small-scale animal hunts and public executions continued. The emperors Leo and Antemius passed legislation in 469 forbidding theatrical shows, chariot races and the hunting of wild animals on feast days.

A particularly violent earthquake at the end of the fifth century caused further damage to the colonnade at the top of the third level of the Colosseum and this collapsed, sending debris crashing into the basement. No attempt was made to restore the upper seating area and what remained of the colonnade was shovelled into the basement and the area filled up with earth. This really marked the final degradation of the Colosseum, though the Romans continued to find a use for the building for a few more decades. The last recorded show in the Colosseum was an animal hunt in 523.

Rome was besieged by the Goths twice more, in 536 and 545, during which time the population suffered famine and plague. When Totila captured the city in 545 he is said to have found no more than 500 people still living there. Such a tiny population had no use for monumental buildings when sheer survival was all that mattered. The revival of the city in the later sixth century resulted in full-scale robbing of the Colosseum for building materials. People removed the travertine blocks, especially from the seating areas, to reuse elsewhere or to make lime mortar. Marble and lead piping were similarly recycled.

The shell of the *cavea* of the Colosseum, especially along the north side, found itself a host to squatters, some of whom converted the vaults into living accommodation and used the radial passages to house their animals and store provisions. Some of the internal stairways were knocked down to create more space. Modern excavations have revealed that a major roadway had been cut through the *cavea* along the line of the main axis to allow wheeled traffic to reach the arena, which had become a goods yard. In addition, 15 minor routes had been created and in some cases walls had been demolished in the process. People also began to colonize the area outside the Amphitheatre, building wooden houses around the perimeter walls.

Pillaging continued on an even larger scale during the second half of the eighth century, when what amounted to systematic quarrying of the site occurred, particularly on the south side, with tunnels being mined for up to 8 metres below the ground so that the masonry of the foundations could be hauled away. Archaeologists have discovered places underground where some of the huge travertine blocks of the foundations have clearly been prised out.

In time, even the iron clamps holding the travertine blocks together were gouged out. At first this occurred mainly at the lower levels where the iron could be easily reached, but later the foragers climbed as far as the third level to get at the iron inside the arches and along the parapet.

By the eighth century the city was at last showing signs of recovery and the authorities started to protect their ancient monuments against such large-scale desecration. The shanty town of wooden houses outside the perimeter walls was demolished and replaced with concrete buildings. These were discovered during the excavations of 1895. Official deeds going back to 7 March 982 show that the land where the arena had once been was transferred to the nearby Church of Santa Maria Nova, who had allowed permanent dwellings to be built there. These houses, as described in the deeds, were typically two storeys high, each with a small garden. They were mostly occupied by artisans, such as bricklayers and stonemasons (the very people who had no doubt been involved in pulverizing the Colosseum's travertine blocks for mortar) as well as cobblers, blacksmiths and coppersmiths. There were also some people of higher status living there, such as money-changers, clergymen and lawyers.

Rome was sacked again in 1084, this time by the Normans. This led to the occupation and fortification of many of the ancient monuments by Rome's noble families. The Colosseum, the Theatre of Marcellus and the Mausoleum of Augustus were all taken over in this way. The Frangipane family fortified the Colosseum and occupied two levels of arches at the eastern end. There is a record of them entertaining Pope Innocent II there. The Annibaldi family took over part of the Frangipane palace in the first half of the thirteenth century and acquired the rest a little later. They were compelled to hand over the building to the Capitoline Senate in 1312 but continued to occupy the premises for another 57 years.

Most of the archaeological evidence for the medieval inhabitation of the Colosseum was removed without being recorded by the early archaeologists, but traces of this occupation still come to light. A detailed examination of three adjoining segments, 44, 45 and 46 (the numbers relate to the entrance numbers inscribed above the outer archways), was recently carried out. The investigators started at the façade and worked in as far as the fourth ring corridor. They examined the spaces below the stairs as well as the radial passages. Their study showed that the area had been used for animal stalls. Traces of three structures, dating from the second half of the twelfth to the beginning of the thirteenth century, were discovered beneath the stairs in sector 46. Recycled materials had been used, including fragments of marble decorations. Two of these fragments were covered with plaster and used as mangers until at least the seventeenth century.

The Colosseum by Angelo Maria Costa (1670–1721), showing the state of the Amphitheatre before the excavations began.

A lead seal belonging to Pope Urban IV (1261–1265) was discovered in the landfill beneath the stairs in segment 45. This relates to the period when the building was occupied by the Frangipane or Annibaldi families.

In 1332 Ludwig of Bavaria visited Rome and the authorities staged a bullfight at the Colosseum in his honour. It was the first time in more than eight hundred years that such an event had been witnessed, so naturally the public turned out to watch in great numbers, though no one, not even the organizers, seems to have realized that this had been one of the Colosseum's original functions. It was to be many years before anyone expressed an interest in the history of Rome's finest ancient monument.

The final catastrophe for the Colosseum occurred in 1349 when Rome was struck by yet another earthquake. Parts of the south and west sides of the *cavea* collapsed, having been considerably weakened by the removal of the stones and the iron clamps that had held them together. Sadly, this disaster seemed to be the cue for yet more desecration and prompted further wholesale quarrying for building materials. In a letter that the Bishop of Orvieto wrote to Pope Urban V in 1362 he complains about the poor response to the sale of travertine blocks from the Colosseum that

he organized. There were plans to restore it as a shrine to the Christian martyrs but these were never carried out and the pillaging continued. The most noticeable effect of this was the total disappearance of the two outer arcades on the southeastern and southwestern sides.

In 1382 the civil government of Rome, the Capitoline Senate, eventually realized that something had to be done and gave the responsibility for maintaining the building to three different authorities: the Church, the Capitoline Senate and the Order of Santissimo Salvatore ad Sancta Sanctorum. Unfortunately, while this move did finally introduce a degree of control, in that it stopped the indiscriminate looting, it did not prevent the removal of the Colosseum's marble and travertine stonework altogether. For the three bodies did not form a joint committee to preserve the building's fabric but allowed materials to be taken away and split the spoils between them. (Inscriptions marking this division can still be seen on the façade.) So now anyone who wanted to obtain their building materials from this source could still do so – they just had to pay the authorities for it.

In the middle of the fifteenth century Pope Eugene IV publicly declared that 'dismantling Rome's ancient monuments meant destroying

The Colosseum seen from the Capitol in a photograph taken in the late nineteenth century, before the columns of the Temple of Venus and Roma were reconstructed. The Arch of Titus is in the foreground and the brick stump to the right of this picture, in front of the Colosseum, is the remains of the Meta Sudans fountain, destroyed to make way for the Via dei Fori Imperiali in 1932.

the very best in the city and the whole world' but he nevertheless allowed its travertine stonework to be used for restoring the nearby Basilica of St John Lateran. His successor, Nicholas V, became the most notorious destroyer of the Colosseum when he robbed it of vast quantities of its stone to make lime mortar for the rebuilding of the Basilica of St Peter in the Vatican, despite the protests of antiquaries such as Poggio Bracciolini, who complained in 1448 that most of the Colosseum had been reduced to lime. The church solved this conflict of interests by placing a preservation order on the north façade and allowing the rest to be quarried.

This ambiguous, if not to say hypocritical, attitude towards the Colosseum was illustrated in the middle of the fifteenth century when Leon Battista Alberti published two books on the ancient buildings of Rome. These created such interest that Pope Nicholas V employed Alberti to submit designs for new buildings. Alberti drew inspiration from the Colosseum, adopting the style of superimposed arcades that became a prototype of Renaissance architecture. But neither Alberti's papal patronage nor his respectful homage to the building was enough to prevent its further destruction.

Successive popes continued their rape of the Colosseum, carrying away more and more of its travertine blocks and marble fittings. Pius II actually had a specially reinforced wagon built for transporting the material. It must be said that it was not just the Colosseum that was being destroyed. All of Rome's ancient monuments suffered the same fate.

In 1585 Pope Sixtus V drew up plans to convert the Colosseum into a spinning mill but the project proved exceedingly expensive and when he died in 1590 the scheme died with him. But maybe the notion of using the building for commerce survived, for four years later a small glue-making cooperative set up in business on the first floor.

Even though the building was now occupied and the land was titled, no attempt was made to maintain it and materials continued to be moved off the site. A document from 1606 refers to the sale of travertine blocks that had fallen from the upper levels of the *cavea*, and when three arches collapsed in 1644 Pope Urban VIII used the fallen masonry in the building of the Barberini Palace.

Pope Clement X planned to put a church dedicated to the Christian martyrs in the arena but it was never built. The project was resurrected by Clement XI at the beginning of the eighteenth century when the Chapel

Buttresses at either end of the surviving section of the outer circuit were constructed in the early nineteenth century. The one at the east side (*left*) was built by Raffaele Stern between 1805 and 1807; the one at the west (*far left*) by Giuseppe Valadier in 1827. A drawing of the time (*below*) shows the latter under construction.

of Santa Maria della Pietà at the northeastern end of the arena was demolished. It is possible that the area was excavated to lay the foundations of the new church, which could account for the destruction of the walls supporting the arena at that end. The idea of building a substantial church in the area was again abandoned, the arches of the north façade were blocked and outer arcades were converted into a manure dump for the production of saltpetre.

Clement XI (1700–21) was the last pope to use the building as a travertine quarry; by the end of his reign official attitudes had at last begun to change although the dumping of manure continued for 70 years, causing devastating corrosion to the travertine pillars, many of which were totally worn away. The plan to convert the arena into a Christian shrine was never totally abandoned and towards the end of his reign Clement XI set up stations of the cross around the arena. The change of attitude was mainly the work of the Capitoline Senate, which had often opposed the church's destructive attitude towards the ancient building.

In 1743 the Senate began restoration work and the following year the governor of Rome passed a law forbidding the desecration of the building. The edict was given teeth by the threat to whip anyone caught damaging the building or even leaving the gates open. The church had agreed to these measures and had even repaired the gates. Finally, in 1749, Pope Benedict XIV dedicated the Colosseum to the Passion of Jesus and pronounced it sanctified by the blood of the martyrs. The era of destruction was over.

It was impossible to repair the damage that had been done to the Colosseum over the centuries but all parties now combined to preserve what was left. Extensive repairs were carried out in the 1760s but very substantial reinforcement was needed at both the east and west ends to stop the outer corridors collapsing. Enclosure walls were built at the first two levels between the arcades and the barrel vaults in 1795 but this was only a stopgap measure. Another earthquake in 1803 forced the authorities to complete the work. Pope Pius VII gave orders for a triangular buttressing wall to be erected at the east end. It took fourteen years to build and was not completed until 1820. The consolidation of the west end was completed a few years later. Restorations continued throughout the nineteenth century but they were now accompanied by extensive excavations both inside and outside. L. Canina consolidated the second ring on the south side, restored part of the north side and rebuilt some of the highest seating level, planning to reconstruct a section of the colonnade, but this was never accomplished.

In 1870 the reunification of Italy, which had been fragmented since the fall of the Roman Empire in the west, created renewed interest in the history of the city. The Office of the Superintendent of the Excavation and Preservation of the Monuments was created to promote excavations in the whole area from the Roman Forum to the Colosseum. The remaining

Benito Mussolini on horseback (centre) at the opening of the Via dei Fori Imperiali in 1932. Several ancient ruins were destroyed to make way for the road.

buildings encroaching on the Colosseum were demolished and the whole area developed, leading to numerous archaeological discoveries.

The earlier part of the twentieth century was marred by the politicization of everything. Although extensive excavations took place they were aimed at glorifying Mussolini's fascist state. The Colosseum became a venue for political demonstrations, causing considerable damage to the building. Stairs were constructed joining the first and second levels, and new asphalt floors were laid to enable the crowds to move more easily. These modifications were destructive and bore no relation to the ancient structures. Botched reconstructions were made during this period, which ignored the evidence. The most destructive development of the fascist era, though it only affected the Colosseum indirectly, was the construction of the Via dei Fori Imperiali which involved cutting through the Velian Hill at the back of the Basilica of Constantine, destroying the ancient remains in the area. The top of the Meta Sudans fountain was removed and the pedestal of Nero's colossal statue was partly destroyed. The building of the Metro also caused considerable damage to the area surrounding the Colosseum as it cut through the ancient drainage system at the west end, causing flooding in the basement. Later, towards the end of the Second World War, the Colosseum was commandeered as a weapons store for German paratroopers.

Sanity returned with the fall of Mussolini but a lot of damage had been done by then. Mussolini's highway delivered ever-increasing traffic into the piazza around the Colosseum and the travertine pavement of the piazza was covered with asphalt. By the 1960s the Colosseum had become marooned on a monumental traffic island and visitors risked their lives trying to negotiate a path across lanes carrying thousands of cars at speed round the site. 'Don't hesitate, walk at a constant pace and the drivers will avoid you,' the locals living in the area advised the sightseers. 'Hesitate and you're dead.'

In the 1980s the City Council agreed to reroute the traffic around the Colosseum, bestowing a modicum of peace and stability to the monument. Visitors can at least now get there without being run over. And the work continues: in 2000 part of the arena floor was restored, giving some protection to the most damaged area of the basement.

Opposite
By the 1960s the Colosseum had become a huge traffic island.

THE EXCAVATIONS

The first official excavation of the Colosseum site took place in the fifteenth century when the ancient drainage system was discovered. It was not until the end of the eighteenth century, however, that systematic surveys were made by Carlo Lucangeli, an Italian engineer who cleared the land-fill and rubble deposited during a thousand years of neglect and uncovered vaults and tunnels in the foundations. The discovery of walls, lifts and long tunnels beneath the arena in the early nineteenth century fired the imagination of successive archaeologists whose painstaking work has helped to complete the picture of exactly what took place in the Amphitheatre.

Opposite
This etching, *The Colosseum from the Southwest*, made by the Flemish artist Jan Gossaert in the winter of 1508–9, is the earliest surviving artistic impression of the building.

For nearly five hundred years, since the last known event at the Colosseum (a wild animal show in AD 523), Rome's famous amphitheatre was allowed to degenerate into a state of decay. Almost immediately looters had begun to strip it of its valuable lead fittings and helped themselves to whatever bits of stone and marble were left lying around. Serious earthquakes in 422 and 508 had caused a lot of damage and there was another one to come in 847. Squatters had been moving in since the tenth century and some of them, like the aristocratic Frangipane family, did some restoration work when it suited their purpose. During this superstitious age people looked upon the Colosseum as a former pagan temple, inhabited by bad spirits, though this attitude did not prevent the vandalism that continued on a massive scale.

As the fabric of the building continued to suffer, the ruin that was the Colosseum became a stark reminder of the past glory of Rome, and in time artists came to look on it as something worthy of commemoration and tourists put it on their list of essential places of historical interest to visit. The Italian poet Petrarch (1304–74), who was an admirer of classical Latin literature and did much to promote it, first visited the Colosseum in 1337, four years before he was crowned Poet Laureate in the city. When he returned to Rome for the last time in 1350 he was shocked to see the damage that yet another earthquake had done the year before.

The earliest known drawing showing the Amphitheatre is a plan of the city of Rome dating from 1320, and the first artistic impression is an etching by the Flemish artist Jan Gossaert. Done in the winter of 1508–09, it shows the building leaning a bit like the Tower of Pisa. There are trees and weeds growing out of the masonry and the ground floor of the *cavea* is buried under a mound of earth.

The first known official investigation of the site took place in the fifteenth century, when archaeologists established where the original ground level had been and so were able to project with almost total accuracy how the façade had looked. They were helped by the fact that some of the structure above ground had survived, especially along the north side of the *cavea*. The really exciting discoveries were made when the excavators dug down and uncovered the ancient subterranean drainage system in the fifteenth century.

It was only in the middle of the seventeenth century that the authorities really faced up to the fact that the Amphitheatre would disappear altogether if they did not put a stop to the systematic quarrying that was

Opposite
A romantic view of
*Excavations inside the
Colosseum* by H. Robert
(1733–1808).

going on. Even so, various popes went on giving themselves permission to take what they wanted from the Colosseum to be re-used in the construction of their grand edifices elsewhere in the city. From the beginning of the eighteenth century, however, the Church became more responsible and eventually the popes took an active interest in the restoration work that was carried out there.

There are no further records of any systematic excavations until 1714, when a shaft was sunk just inside the surviving remains of the *cavea*. The excavators dug down for 5.68 metres to reach the travertine paving of one of the tunnels, which was assumed to be the floor of the arena. Restoration on a minor scale was carried out for the next 75 years or so but there were no important discoveries made during this period. It was not until the 1790s that more serious work was carried out, by Carlo Lucangeli, an Italian engineer. By this time the landfill outside the Colosseum was almost 4 metres deep in places and the inner ring corridor that gave access to the senators' ringside seats was totally blocked. Lucangeli hired gangs of labourers to clear the rubble from the upper vaults of the *cavea* and supervised the excavation of the lower two levels.

In 1805 the Church's Commissioner of Antiquity, Abbot Carlo Fea, put forward a proposal to Pope Pius VII for a much more extensive programme of excavation and Lucangeli was co-opted to work alongside the official architects and archaeologists assigned to the project. The authorities placed around 160 prisoners at their disposal to do the donkey work involved in excavating the ground floor. They uncovered the complex drainage system just below the travertine pavement both inside and outside the *cavea*. Vaults under the steps were cleared and Lucangeli and Fea confidently declared them to be latrines and brothels. They also uncovered a vaulted tunnel in the southeastern sector of the arena that had been cut through the concrete foundations in the latter half of the second century AD. This tunnel, which has a stuccoed ceiling and is richly decorated with wall paintings, emerges in the senatorial seating area and it was suggested that this was the route that the emperor Commodus would have taken to enter the arena. Certainly the wall paintings in this section can be dated to his era.

Work was interrupted briefly when Napoleon invaded the Papal States in 1807 but his enthusiasm for archaeology ensured that no damage was done to the site. And in fact French archaeologists started working on the excavation alongside the Italians in 1811. They were responsible for clearing the north

Part of Carlo Lucangeli's incredible cork model of the Colosseum, now in the Ecole des Beaux-Arts, Paris.

side of the piazza and built a buttress wall along the foot of the hill to prevent a landslide.

Lucangeli spent 22 years working on the Colosseum and for much of this time he had no official position but continued the excavations at his own expense. He was a master model-maker and he produced a superbly detailed three-dimensional cork model (at a scale of 1:60) of the Amphitheatre as it appeared after ten years of excavation work. The Ecole des Beaux-Arts in Paris purchased the model in 1809 and it remains a lasting tribute to his dedication. A second model, in wood, was completed by his son-in-law, Paolo Dalbono, and is on display at the Colosseum. Shortly before his death in 1812 Lucangeli was made a custodian of the Colosseum in recognition of his contribution to the task of unravelling the mysteries of Rome's most famous monument.

Up to this point it was generally believed that the earth-fill in the centre of the arena covered an elliptical brick-lined pit, which could be flooded to fight the sea-battles as described by Martial and Cassius Dio. It seemed that this theory would be disproved when the French excavators uncovered a mass of walls filling the arena. They exposed the upper part of these substructures, finding the vaulted chambers along the north side that housed the lifts in the perimeter wall. These were excavated to well below the level of the travertine consoles. Virtually all the crucial elements were revealed, including the sloping half arches along the sides of the central corridor and all the later lift shafts in the adjacent passages. The arguments about the possibility of staging sea-battles in the Colosseum raged on. Were these the original Roman walls or were they later additions, possibly medieval? If the walls were Roman then there could not have been a *naumachia* in the Colosseum. In 1812 the Italian architect Bianchi managed to prove that the walls dated from the Roman period but not everyone was convinced.

Between 1811 and 1814 the French excavators penetrated deep into the long axis tunnels at both ends of the Colosseum. At the west end they explored the tunnel until it turned north beneath the piazza outside the building, discovering the deep annular drainage channel running some 8 metres below the pavement along the perimeter. The saturated ground made the work increasingly difficult, and when they located a manhole near the site of the chapel of Santa Maria della Pietà on the edge of the arena they were forced to abandon the dig at a depth of 3.5 metres because the area was flooded. The west tunnel has never been re-excavated. Following rumours of buried treasure, the access tunnel on the south side was opened up but nothing of value was found there.

Napoleon's European empire collapsed in 1814 and the French withdrew from Rome. No further attempt was made to excavate the basement for another half century. The French architect Louis-Joseph Duc had studied Lucangeli's cork model at the Ecole des Beaux-Arts before going to Rome to see the Colosseum for the first time. He made a series of coloured drawings of the Amphitheatre in around 1829-30. These show in great detail the condition of the building and he also sketched out his ideas of how it might have looked originally. Fortunately, Duc also studied the excavated structures in the basement, so providing an invaluable record of the state of many of the subterranean areas. His drawings show that the basement had once more flooded, with a water level 3.5 metres below the arena. The basement was filled in at a later date to preserve the ancient structures.

In 1864-65 treasure hunters carried out more extensive excavations between the Colosseum and the Caelian Hill. They unintentionally managed to flood the whole area as far as the Arch of Constantine when they breached an underground water source, and the distinguished Italian archaeologist Rodolfo Lanciani was drafted in to sort the mess out. When he excavated below the ancient pavement in this area he opened up an old drain to find it had been blocked with Christian lamps and the skulls and bones of bears, lions and tigers.

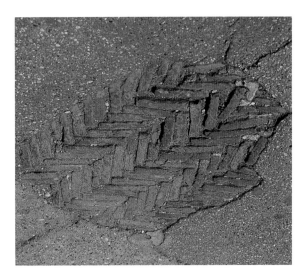

Part of the original herringbone brick floor is visible on the first level through the asphalt added in the early twentieth century.

Excavations began again in earnest in 1874, at the eastern end of the arena. This time the diggers reached the herringbone brick floor (*opus spiccatum*) of the basement and they also uncovered the entrance to the main axial drain. Once again the work created more flooding in the area and the water had to be pumped out. It was during this time that the graffito (page 195) was found which seemed to show the old lift shafts set into the perimeter wall with the floor of the arena some 2 metres below its later level.

In 1876 John Henry Parker, the curator of the Ashmolean Museum in Oxford, published the results of this excavation. His book *The Archaeology of Rome: The Colosseum* is crucial to the study of the building as it contains photographs and drawings of certain artefacts now lost, but his interpretation of the data must be read critically. He was convinced, for instance, that much of what he saw, especially the vaulted chambers in the perimeter wall, was built during Nero's time and he claimed that the tufa walls were even earlier. However, he did accurately identify the lift shafts in the corridor around the perimeter of the arena. By this time, of course, the Colosseum was a popular tourist destination, as he observed:

> The excavations of 1874 and 1875 very much astonished the people
> of Rome, and more especially the English visitors who had been long
> accustomed to consider the 'area' and the arena to be the same thing;
> they were amazed to see the whole of the 'area' undermined by walls.

A photograph of the central corridor taken at the time of the 1874–75 excavations showing the wooden flooring (now lost) in the Colosseum basement.

Excavation beneath the piazza surrounding the Colosseum continued throughout the latter quarter of the nineteenth century and the drainage system was further revealed. One dig, in 1881, at the southeastern end, broke into the tunnel leading to the Ludus Magnus and the drain beneath it.

By this time excavators had uncovered the foundations of the complete eastern half of the basement, much of which had been almost totally destroyed at some earlier period. They had explored along the perimeter wall in the northern sector and had made a detailed study of the vaulted chambers and the shafts behind them. They had also penetrated into the eastern tunnel, clearing the rooms on either side and the two lower lying galleries, continuing for some distance under the piazza. The area beneath the tunnel was also excavated and Parker reports: 'There are evident marks of a great flood-gate or sluice drawn up, as a portcullis, at the entrance to this drain.'

The excavation of the eastern end of the central long axis corridor uncovered about 25.5 metres of wooden boarding complete with 44 joists at intervals of 2 Roman feet (about 60 centimetres). At the time this was described as a cradle for a galley to be used in the *naumachia*, but later scholars believe it is more likely to have been a gangway raised above the silted up floor because of the frequent flooding. Unfortunately, the structure soon disappeared and even the most basic facts, such as the exact dimensions and what type of wood it was, were never published.

The western end of the arena was not excavated until 1938–39, when an Italian engineer, Giuseppe Cozzo, began clearing the area. Cozzo had been involved in the study of the basement for more than forty years and had published a book, *Ingegneria Romana*, in 1928. This included an invaluable section outlining his theories on the construction of the Colosseum. He re-examined the basement and corrected many of Parker's dating errors. He also identified the original animal lifts set into the perimeter wall, though he failed to realize that these could only have functioned before the tufa pillars were built in front of them. Cozzo's results have to be viewed with some caution, however, for his excavation reports, which were never published, show that he was responsible for demolishing more than 1,600 cubic metres of masonry that he considered unstable.

Cozzo began his excavation by clearing the central corridor underneath the arena, where he found housings for the machinery that had been used for raising heavy scenery (*pegmata*). His reconstruction of how this part of the

A schematic drawing of the excavation of the central corridor H of the basement showing the remains of an earlier tufa building (A) which was levelled off and covered by a concrete foundation 40 centimetres thick (B) and a herringbone brick-work floor above it (C).

Colosseum functioned is still accepted by most experts today. When archaeologists re-examined the central corridor in 1975 they discovered that the foundations of the two walls on either side were at least 1.4 metres below the brick floor and that the floor itself was built on top of a 40-centimetre thick concrete base. These sturdy foundations, both of the walls and the corridor itself, support the view that the *pegmata* was located here. This later excavation also uncovered the whole width of the central corridor at its western end for a distance of 2–3 metres. At this point, to their astonishment, the excavators uncovered the northwestern corner of a substantial building made of tufa blocks. It was estimated that this structure predated the Colosseum by at least a century.

Archaeologists have always wanted to know exactly where Nero's lake had been, and this discovery looked as though it would provide the answer. The remains of the tufa stone building were an estimated 4–5 metres below the level of the surrounding area, so the assumption is that it was knocked down and the site levelled off to form the bed of the lake. There was one thing that the excavators definitely proved: the area was naturally prone to flooding. Their test trench quickly filled with water and they had to keep pumping it out. Unfortunately, this meant that they could not dig down any deeper.

Cozzo went on to clear the passageways that flanked the central corridor, with their later lift shafts, until he finally came to the vaulted chambers in the perimeter wall. This area was blocked with rubble, which he had removed. Here parts of the colonnaded portico and other fragments of the *cavea* were found in heaps. In the southwestern sector he discovered a part of the curved tufa wall that was almost intact right up to the level of the arena, so revealing all the details of how the lifts functioned. However, he found that the structures beneath the ceremonial entrance for the gladiators were almost totally destroyed and, against all the principles of good archaeological practice, he cleared the site and totally rebuilt the area, covering it with a concrete ceiling. His reconstructive work along the top of the containing wall was equally damaging. He removed many of the surviving travertine blocks in a totally arbitrary manner, thus compromising the stability of the vaulted chambers underneath. In recent years some of his alterations have been reversed and modern scientific methods have managed to rectify what he did, though some of the data he originally uncovered has been lost for ever.

While Cozzo was excavating the basement of the Colosseum in the late 1930s the authorities were allowing yet more destruction to take place outside the building, with the construction of the Metropolitana, the new

Excavations made in 1939 during the construction of the Metropolitana, Rome's underground railway system, cut across ancient drains which can be seen in the sides of this trench dug at the west end of the Colosseum piazza.

The Ludus Magnus was discovered in 1937 and excavated in the late 1950s.

underground railway system. Work started with a huge trench being dug across the northwestern side of the piazza that almost touched the foundations of the Arch of Constantine and came to within 8 metres of the Colosseum itself. While it just about avoided the building, the trench cut right into the ancient Roman sewerage system. And although they were unable to halt this underground destruction, the archaeologists were at least allowed in to examine the drains. The main drain connecting with the conduit emerging from the basement was particularly interesting. It was built of brick and, because the Romans stamped their bricks, they were easily identified. The materials in this case dated back to the reign of Domitian. This is particularly intriguing as it raises the question of how the basement was drained at the time of Titus. An examination of the point where the conduit of the Vespasianic period emerged from the Amphitheatre produced another surprise, showing that the conduit had accommodated a two-way system carrying water both in and out of the basement. (Refer to the plan on page 192.)

The Ludus Magnus was discovered during building operations in 1937. The site was left open but excavation did not start until 1957. Over the next four years about half the school was uncovered, leaving the rest of the remains beneath the road and buildings to the south. The excavations showed that although the building was started by Domitian it was not completed until the time of Hadrian.

There were only a few minor investigations of the Colosseum in the last quarter of the twentieth century. Between 1973 and 1977 archaeologists examined the conduits at the northern and southern ends of the short axis and these were the first totally scientific excavations.

By the sixth century AD, by which time the Romans had stopped using the Colosseum as an entertainment venue, the short axis drain on the south and north sides had silted up to the point where it was totally blocked. At some time after it had become blocked it was walled off with bricks. The silting-up laid down various strata, some of which contained archaeological material, the pure silt being deposited when the Amphitheatre was out of use.

In amongst the various layers of silt the excavators uncovered some three thousand animal and bird bones – from lions, panthers, bears, deer, horses, donkeys, pigs, cows and sheep, and chickens, swans, geese and birds of prey – together with shards of pottery and small personal items like dice and hairpins. They also found the shells of limpets and oysters and the stones of fruit such as peaches, cherries, plums and olives, all of which had been discarded by the spectators to be washed down through the drains into the basement when it rained. The presence of bones both in these drains and in the main drain some 300 metres further down the system (first opened by Rodolfo Lanciani in the nineteenth century) suggests that the animals killed in the arena were dumped in the basement drains, or maybe the meat was eaten by the slaves operating the machinery beneath the arena and they discarded the bones, which finished up in the drains.

In June 1986 a trench was dug on the southeastern side of the Colosseum by Italgas to lay a gas main which clipped the edge of the site immediately south of the eastern entrance. A team of rescue archaeologists immediately took over and managed to examine the upper part of the brick-faced foundations. The gas trench cut through the upper annular drain which was brick lined with a pent roof made from two *bipedales*, the two-foot square flat Roman bricks (1 Roman foot equals approximately

30 centimetres). The results of this investigation have not been fully published yet but one interesting feature has emerged: the brick-cased concrete containing the drain appears to have been added on to the outside of the brick-faced concrete of the foundations, possibly indicating two separate building periods.

Excavations just north of the Arch of Constantine during the 1980s uncovered a portico belonging to Nero's Golden Palace, which extended under the western part of the Colosseum. This again raised speculation as to the exact location of Nero's lake, but it is difficult to reject Martial's statement: 'Where rises before our eyes the noble structure of the Amphitheatre, was once Nero's lake.' One must assume that the portico bordered the lake. It would be difficult to imagine the circumstances under which the remains of the late Republican tufa building discovered at a depth of 1.5 metres beneath the basement floor could have been left in situ for any other reason than that they were on the bed of the lake. Further investigations have taken place beneath the basement floor recently, revealing more traces of late Republican buildings, including a black and white mosaic floor dating to about 100 BC.

The Colosseum is possibly the most studied building in Rome, but many details are still unknown. The problem of how water was introduced into the building remains uncertain. (This is discussed in detail in Appendix I.) There have been several substantial studies published in the latter half of the twentieth century. In particular one should mention C. Mocchegiani Carpano and R. Luciani's *I restauri dell'Anfiteatro Flavio* (1981) and an archaeological survey of the southwestern sector of the basement by the Netherlands Institute in Rome (1991). Currently Heinz-Jurgen Beste is making a detailed survey of the basement complete with plans and sections at a scale of 1:25. Only a few details of this vast enterprise have so far been published.

APPENDIX I
BENEATH THE ARENA

THE BASEMENT AT THE TIME OF TITUS

THE AXIAL TUNNELS

The containing wall of the basement of the Colosseum is divided into four by tunnels leading to outside facilities. One of these tunnels led to the Ludus Magnus and two came up in the piazza, but the destination of the other is unknown. The short axis tunnels leading to the north and south are about 3.3 metres wide and 5.3 metres high but in each the floor has been raised about 1.2 metres to accommodate a water conduit beneath the floor. The long axis tunnels are also raised about 1.2 metres to accommodate a water conduit underneath but are far more complex.

The east tunnel, built of well-cut travertine blocks, is very well preserved. It is about 3.3 metres wide at the entrance, opening out into a fan-shaped area accommodating four rooms at the same level, two on each side of the passage. Two stairways lead from the small front rooms up to the level of the arena. The fan-shaped area is flanked by two galleries about 24 metres long at the same level as the basement floor and opening onto it. Six travertine capstan blocks, some with the remains of bronze collars (presumably for removable capstans) are set into the floor of each of the galleries. These two galleries were joined by a tunnel running at the higher level along the back of the fan-shaped area. Doorways from the four rooms also gave access to the galleries. The axial passage extends beyond the fan-shaped area and is flanked by four more rooms, two on either side, before entering a partially cleared vaulted tunnel just under 2 metres wide apparently connecting the basement to the Ludus Magnus.

At the west end there appears to have been a similar arrangement, though it is poorly preserved. The north side of the fan-shaped area is severely damaged, but there were two rooms on the south side with a

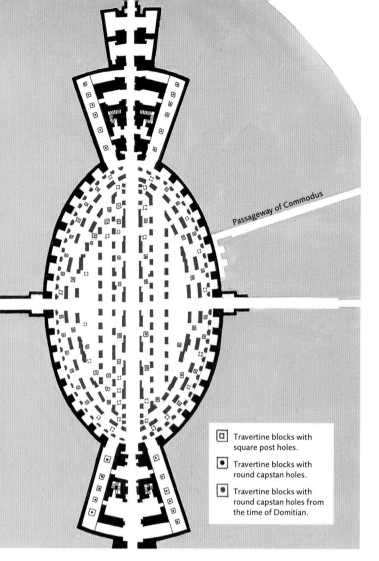

Plan of the basement of the Colosseum. The structures at the time of Titus are shown in black and the modifications of the time of Domitian are shown in red.

Passageway of Commodus

☐ Travertine blocks with square post holes.

☐ Travertine blocks with round capstan holes.

☐ Travertine blocks with round capstan holes from the time of Domitian.

'spiral' staircase built into the dividing wall and entered from the larger back room. A connecting passage and doorways from the rooms, similar to those at the eastern end, open onto the lower-lying galleries. The early nineteenth-century excavators penetrated beyond the fan-shaped area, reaching a point just outside the building, where the tunnel turned north before rising to the level of the piazza.

THE VAULTED CHAMBERS

The four tunnels divide the basement perimeter wall into four sectors each indented by eight shallow vaulted compartments 2.95 metres wide, 1.6 metres deep and 5.3 metres high. They are similar to the chambers in Hellenistic curtain walls. The brick facing of the perimeter wall at the level of the vault has generally disappeared and what remains is of a later date. Originally it had been built out further towards the centre of the basement with a wedge-shaped hole in the top of the vault. This was filled in when the wall was cut back. The rear wall of each compartment is pierced by a small aperture, 80 centimetres wide and 110 centimetres high, with its threshold about 2.65 metres above floor level, leading to a shaft 90 centimetres square and 3 metres high, emerging at the level of the arena.

The vaulted chambers are separated by a wall 1.8 metres wide, which juts out 60 centimetres beyond the present face of the perimeter wall. The base of this extension is built of brick, but at a height of about 1.10 metres a large travertine block, 75-100 centimetres in height and about 70 centimetres in depth, stretching the whole width of the dividing wall, has been inserted. Above this, the brick wall continues for another metre but it is now split into two rectangular pilasters, with a gap of 44 centimetres between them, each topped with a travertine console about 2 metres long and 60 centimetres deep and the same width as the brick pilaster. The console is set into the main

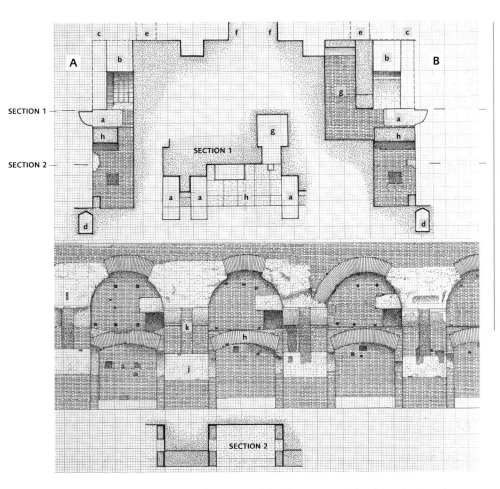

The shallow vaulted chambers along the perimeter wall of the basement in the northwest sector. The upper part of the wall, above the travertine consoles, was cut back at the time of Domitian and the wedge-shaped hole (b) at the apex of the vault was bricked in. The wall surrounding the arena (e) was moved back to allow more space around the arena (f). The mezzanine floor (h), dividing the chamber in two, was also a later addition.

A Left side of the chamber
B Right side of the chamber with section through the shaft at the back (g)
a Travertine console
b Wedge-shaped hole
c Original face of the upper level of the perimeter wall
d Drainage channel
e Original position of the wall surrounding the arena
f Later position of the wall surrounding the arena
g Vertical shaft behind the vaulted chamber
h Mezzanine floor
j Load-bearing travertine block supporting the cantilever system on which the original floor of the arena rested
k Slot for the upright timber of the cantilever system

body of the perimeter wall and extends 40 centimetres beyond the face of the brick pilaster. Both the travertine block and the consoles are clearly load-bearing. The back of the trough between the brick pilasters is set out about 15 centimetres from the present level of the upper part of the perimeter wall.

The basement perimeter wall briefly described above is an integral part of the *cavea*. It is built of the same materials and is unquestionably of the

The entrance to the north short axis tunnel and the water conduit beneath it.

same date. Nothing else in the basement is of this date – it is all from a later period. The earliest internal structures of the basement are built of tufa. Not only are they demonstrably later but they also show a complete change of function, rendering the travertine consoles between the vaulted chambers redundant; in fact, at the northwestern and southeastern ends they are actually built into the tufa of the later phase. Although the vaulted compartments were adapted to a new function, being divided into an upper and lower level, the floor dividing the two levels partially blocks off the aperture leading to the vertical shaft behind the back wall, reducing its height to a little over 60 centimetres. All the evidence suggests that during the earliest period of the Colosseum the basement consisted of a brick-lined pit 44.07 metres wide, 76.12 metres long and 6.57 metres deep, with no internal structures whatsoever.

EVIDENCE FOR THE *NAUMACHIA*

I remember visiting the Colosseum for the first time in 1964 and wandering round the inside of the building looking down at the complex system of walls that once supported the wooden flooring of the arena. One could easily distinguish several different building materials; brick predominated but there was also light brown volcanic tufa and the occasional piece of white travertine. The walls were scored with a mass of incomprehensible

A reconstruction of the basement at the time of Titus showing the lifts in the vaulted chambers along the perimeter wall, the cantilever system and the wooden piles used to support the arena.

ruts and slots, mute witnesses to the activity that went on below the arena. As I stood there, imagining what it must have been like to work down there, a group of English-speaking tourists moved up next to me and I heard their guide say, 'Mock sea-battles were fought here.' I also heard another voice mumble, 'Oh yeah, pull the other leg.'

A *naumachia* usually featured certain scenic effects. One of these was a wooden hill that formed an island in the middle of the flooded area, which normally had a painted wooden fort on it. This fort would have been placed beneath the island and then jacked up into position by men working underneath. The island would have large gaps in its base to let the water flow under it. It is possible to estimate the dimensions of this structure in the basement of the Colosseum very accurately as its corner towers had to correspond with the posts that supported the arena. Three of the four travertine blocks into which the piles would have been slotted have been identified here. They form a rectangle measuring 8 × 5 metres. It could not have been any bigger than this as the boats had to be able to manoeuvre.

There is further evidence in the basement to suggest that it could have been flooded for a *naumachia*. Traces of *opus signinum*, the plaster-like cement used for waterproofing, have been found lining the brick facing of the perimeter wall at various points throughout the southern half of the basement. The raised level of the fan-shaped areas with their lower-lying

A reconstruction of the fan-shaped area at the eastern end of the basement, which may have been used for housing ships for the *naumachia*.

flanking tunnels, the raised entrances to the shafts behind the vaulted compartments and the four oversized water channels all support the hypothesis that it would have been possible to flood the basement in a controlled way.

The two 24-metre-long flanking galleries at either end of the long axis tunnels could have been ship sheds for shallow-draught galleys. The floor slopes slightly down towards the arena (dropping 20 centimetres from back to front) with a shallow drainage channel down either side. It is about a metre below the level of the fan-shaped area at the back and 1.15 metres at the doorway near the front. The fan-shaped area could have served as a quay from which the galley could be boarded. But this would only work if the water were no more than 1.2 metres deep; above this the passages on both axes would flood. A depth of 1.2 metres would be sufficient for Roman horses 12–14 hands in height to be forced to swim as described by Cassius Dio and for the operation of shallow draught galleys of the Lake Nemi type. However, it would have been more impressive with deeper water. If it was possible to flood the basement reasonably quickly then the sailors could board the boats before the water reached the level of the axial passages; they would then rise with the water. Each flanking tunnel could house either two galleys 10 metres long and between 2 and 3 metres wide, or one considerably larger one. The smaller galleys could accommodate eight rowers a side.

There is a serious objection to a water level of 1.2 metres because only two thirds of the area would be visible to spectators opposite the short axis

THE HENLEY COLLEGE LIBRARY

and three quarters to those opposite the long axis. To increase the depth of the water would require watertight doors closing the tunnels. Unfortunately, the entrances to all four tunnels are now so badly damaged that all evidence has been lost, but such things were not beyond the capabilities of Roman engineers.

THE SUPPLY AND DRAINAGE OF WATER

If one completely ignores the possibility of a *naumachia* within the Colosseum, one is still left with the problem of how the water for supplying the large number of fountains and latrines within the building was piped in. The Italian engineer Leonardo Lombardi, in his article on the water system of the Colosseum, points to the large number of vertical channels in the internal walling of the building, arguing that half of these must have been for inflow pipes which operated on a siphon system from a large cistern on the Caelian Hill to the south. We know that there was definitely a cistern there dating from the third century AD but the fact that Claudius had built a temple on the hill, which Nero later converted into a *nymphaeum*, a decorative fountain, would suggest that there was an earlier cistern there. The site was supplied with water that came via the Claudian aqueduct, which was completed in AD 52, not long before the Colosseum was built. Excavators digging in an area between the Colosseum and the Caelian Hill in 1864-65 broke into an underground water conduit and managed to flood the piazza as far as the Arch of Constantine.

We may assume that there was a similar cistern on the Esquiline Hill to the northeast, supplying Nero's Golden Palace and later the Baths of Titus. Such a cistern certainly existed a quarter of a century later to supply Trajan's Baths. This cistern, known as Sette Sale, was long considered to be a part of the Golden Palace complex because its orientation was the same as the palace, but a recent archaeological survey has shown that it was built at the time of Trajan. However, it is possible that Trajan rebuilt an earlier cistern on the same site, which would account for its orientation. The two cisterns would have had a maximum elevation of 30 metres above the Colosseum piazza and therefore could not have supplied tanks at a higher level than the second floor of the building. There might also have been a third cistern supplied by the Labican Stream before it joined the sewers. Such cisterns could well have been used to flood the basement, though it is impossible with our present knowledge of the water conduits beneath the piazza to establish how the water got from the cisterns to the basement of the Colosseum.

The drainage system of the Colosseum has been carefully studied and well researched over the centuries. The whole building was designed like a giant funnel, channelling all the rainwater into the basement beneath the arena. It has been estimated that in a heavy downpour 175 litres of water a second would reach the basement. This volume could be easily discharged through the four large drainage conduits leading from the basement to the main drainage system outside the Amphitheatre. The north and south conduits were examined in 1973-77. The south drain is 1.8 metres high and 1.3 metres wide with a pent roof. The north drain is slightly smaller: 1.4 metres high and 1.2 metres wide. Both slope outwards at an angle of about 1:40.

Just outside the Amphitheatre the early excavators discovered two drains running round the entire building at different levels. The upper drain, at a depth of 2 metres, collected water from the upper part of the building and from outside the Amphitheatre. It was connected by a series of vertical overflows to a larger drain at a depth of 8 metres. The lower drain, measuring 55 centimetres wide and 1.5 metres deep, was connected to the four radial conduits coming out of the basement. The water was then carried to the main drain, running beneath what is now the Via di S. Giorgio and ultimately discharging into the Tiber. The outer drainage system beneath the Colosseum piazza has been located at many points over the last two centuries. The system is exceedingly complex and is still not completely understood. It incorporates drains from an earlier period and one at the west end built after the opening of the Colosseum. The west conduit had been adapted just outside the building to operate an outflow and inflow system. It is possible that the north and south conduits, which have only been partially

Plan of the drains in and around the Colosseum. The drains are shown in blue. The route of the Metropolitana railway is shown in red. *Insets* A: Section of the long axis main drain. B: Section of the upper and lower annular drains. C: Section of the short axis main drain.

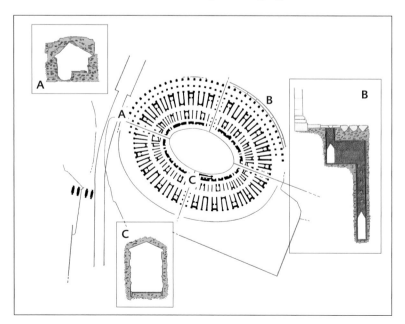

excavated, might show the same feature. When the south drain was examined in the 1970s the excavators found that the floor had been relaid at the time of Domitian, suggesting a possible change of function.

The junctions of the north and south radial conduits with the deep annular drain have never been examined but there is some evidence to suggest that the conduits continued beyond the 8-metre annular drain.

Most archaeologists have rejected the idea that four radial conduits could be used to flood the basement, arguing that as the drains slope outwards they were designed for drainage. This is of course true. And modern hydraulic engineers agree that the problem the original designers of the Colosseum had, bearing in mind where it was built, was how to keep it drained. Anyone who has been down into the basement will remember it as a dank, unhealthy place, where, as an American colleague once put it, 'it will flood of its own accord'. This was the experience of the early excavators and nothing has changed. A hole dug in the floor of the basement will fill with water within hours. It was therefore necessary that the water conduits should be primarily designed to drain the basement, but the fact that they have an outward slope of 1:40 does not preclude their being used to flood the basement with water coming from the much higher altitude of the hills to the north and south.

I presented this working hypothesis to a drainage engineer, John Elms, who has experience of working in the Fens in eastern England, and posed the question: how long would it take to flood the basement to a depth of 1.2 metres, allowing for a drop of approximately 30 metres over a distance of about 200 metres from cisterns on the Caelian and Esquiline Hills, coupled with a supposed Labican reservoir? Elms gave an astonishing answer: four minutes. Theoretically. He warned that it might cause considerable damage. When I asked him about the upward slope of the conduit he replied immediately that it would help to slow the water down. Using all four conduits he estimated that the basement could be drained in less than half an hour.

So theoretically it would have been possible to introduce water into the Amphitheatre through the four radial drains, but no evidence for conduits connecting the main drainage system to a water supply has ever been found. Having said that, one must consider the limitations of the evidence. Suetonius and Cassius Dio offer little help as they give us no idea of the state of the area surrounding the Colosseum in the summer of AD 80, but

Martial actually refers to scaffolding, implying that work was ongoing. It is generally accepted that the building was unfinished at the time of the opening but to what extent is not known. Did the area still have the appearance of a building site? We know that the gladiator schools Ludus Magnus and the Ludus Dacicus were built later. Given such uncertainty one must accept the possibility of temporary wood-lined aqueducts connected to the unfinished drainage system. There certainly must have been such a temporary drain at the west end predating the later brick drain, but no trace of it has ever been found. We cannot even be sure that the flooding of the Colosseum was not restricted to its opening and then abandoned. Archaeology often offers details of an overall picture in which it can be shown that one element predates or postdates another but can very seldom provide a precise dating.

If we assume for a moment that it *was* possible to introduce water through the main radial drains, then by the most conservative estimate the basement could be flooded or drained in less than half an hour. The process would require sluice gates at the cisterns, at the points of entrance into the basement and where the temporary conduits joined the main radial drains. There is one very pertinent question: why is the capacity of the deep outside drain less than that of the smallest of the main radial drains when the outer drain had to cope with a far greater volume of water? Could the answer be that the four radial drains were designed to cope with a massive inflow when the basement was flooded?

Some scholars have suggested that the basement could be flooded using the internal rainwater drainage system in the *cavea* but this does not solve the problem of getting sufficient water to the Amphitheatre in order to do it quickly. It also presents enormous problems, as the internal drainage system is cumulative, increasing in capacity as it gets lower, and even if such a system could be used it would be very slow. The system would require large cisterns at the highest possible level of the *cavea*. These probably did exist to supply the fountains and latrines at the first, second and third levels but their capacity would not be sufficient to supply the 3 million litres of water required to flood the basement to a depth of 1.2 metres. However, it would be visually exciting to incorporate this system into the flooding process with water coming down the shafts at the back of the vaulted chambers and cascading into the basement.

BOARDING OVER

The original elements of the containing wall, which became redundant when the line of tufa pillars was built, are clearly related to the boarding over of the basement. The travertine blocks and consoles seem to be designed to support cantilevered beams projecting out into the arena. At a maximum distance of 6–7 metres these would need to be supported by upright posts. There is a series of travertine blocks in corridor C (see plan of basement, page 186). All have a square hole in the middle the same width as the space between the consoles (43 × 43 centimetres). They are about 6 metres from the containing wall and positioned opposite the consoles. Heinz-Jurgen Beste estimated where two others should be located and excavations confirmed his guess. We may therefore assume there were such features opposite most, if not all, of the consoles. A series of square postholes has been discovered beneath the later brick wall across the two D-shaped areas, another 5 metres into the basement, but these may have been for a wooden partition. In corridor G there are four travertine blocks similar to those in corridor C. If these are for wooden piles then the north and south sections could each be spanned by three joists 5–7 metres long. This is an exceedingly long span, requiring some support in the middle. Certainly there is evidence for a cantilever system in the perimeter wall. This system of supporting piles would leave a 7-metre wide central aisle, possibly left open for the scenic devices (*pegmata*). Constructing the arena would require thousands of wooden parts, piles, beams, prefabricated trapdoors and floorboards plus innumerable wooden pegs. All must have been numbered and divided into sets earmarked for certain areas. The various zones in the basement would have needed to be fenced off to prevent the wild animals from escaping.

The arena at this early period must have been level with the top of the basement's perimeter wall, as it was when the internal structures were built at the time of Domitian. However, a graffito found in 1874 appears to show the upper part of the perimeter wall, with the vaulted chambers closed with grilles and a barrier protecting spectators from the wild animals above them. It also seems to suggest that the arena was initially at a lower level but may only show what the viewer could see during a *naumachia*.

Fragment from a marble slab found during the excavations of 1874–75 showing part of the front of the podium. This graffito by an unknown spectator is the only depiction of the niches and service doors that were originally in the wall surrounding the arena. The vaulted chambers are shown closed with grilles, and above them the framework of a barrier protecting the spectators from the wild animals.

THE MODIFICATIONS OF DOMITIAN

We do not know the reason but Domitian decided to abandon the *naumachia* in the Colosseum and install permanent structures beneath the arena, probably in the mid-AD 80s. Though often obscured by subsequent repairs, shoring up and restructuring, his alterations are easily identifiable as they were done with blocks of tufa, the soft brownish stone used to build the Servian Wall. However, it seems that Domitian drastically altered the original plan. The new structures consisted of a series of walls 90 centimetres thick, the remains of which can be seen all over the basement today, although much of the original stonework has been encased in brick or destroyed altogether. Furthermore, the excavation of the eastern end in 1874-75 appears to have been hasty and so, unfortunately, much of the evidence has been lost forever. Assuming that the design was symmetrical, however, it is possible to deduce what the rest of it looked like even before Beste's survey and reconstruct the substructures beneath the arena as they were in the time of Domitian in almost every detail.

Right Travertine block with a square hole.

A reconstruction of the basement at the time of Domitian showing the tufa walls supporting the arena and the new lift system in corridor B.

The new permanent arena rested on six straight walls parallel to the main axis and three elliptical walls running parallel to the perimeter wall. These walls created corridors in which the hidden machinery of the arena operated. As the basement floor consisted only of a 40-centimetre-thick layer of concrete, faced with bricks laid in herringbone fashion, resting on the demolished buildings of the previous century, deep foundations, at least for the walls on either side of the long axis, had to be inserted. These were essential to enable heavy scenic machinery to be operated in this area. In other areas Domitian's builders appear made no real attempt to sink deep foundations but set shallow strips of concrete into the existing floor and built the light tufa walls on top of them. Within a short time, perhaps as little a ten years, these walls began to collapse and had to be shored up with brickwork. Brick stamps show that this patching up began before the end of the first century. More shoring up took place at the time of Trajan and still more at the end of the second century when the lower half of several of the walls had to be encased in brick.

Domitian's engineers appear originally to have planned just two walls parallel to the perimeter wall running the whole way round the basement. The outermost wall was just under 3.5 metres from the perimeter wall and the second was 3 metres further in. Both walls were pierced by a series of broad arches to allow easy movement. One of the arches in each wall was aligned with the short axis to create a north–south central corridor. There was a 4-metre break in the walls where they crossed the long axis to create a long axis corridor. The system of curved and straight walls left a large D-shaped area between the inner curved wall and the outer straight wall. That this was all part of a single concept is proved by the existence of narrow doorways left in the curved walls to give access to the corridors formed by the parallel straight walls.

At some point it was decided to abandon the lift shafts set into the perimeter wall and place them next to the first of the new curved walls. The upper part of the old shafts was cut back, possibly to allow a narrow wooden walkway halfway up the wall, and a line of massive stone piers was built in front of them rendering them useless. This line of piers capped with a stone lintel ran the whole way round the arena leaving gaps for access at the four tunnels. Twenty-eight or possibly thirty-two lifts were installed in the narrow 2-metre-wide space between the new tufa wall and the line of pillars. Thirty-two lifts would seem to be the more likely figure as the whole building is based on multiples of eight. This would be exactly the same number as those previously housed in the

The basement of the Colosseum showing the line of tufa piers forming the outside of corridor B in the background. Note the fittings for the ramps leading to the arena cut into the lintels.

perimeter wall. The corridors formed by the curved and straight walls are now identified with letters, 'A' being the outer curved corridor and 'H' the main central corridor.

The placing of the line of tufa piers in front of the vaulted chambers, in places actually touching the travertine consoles set into the perimeter wall, proves without a doubt that the original lift shafts had been abandoned. Traces of the new lift system can be clearly detected in the northwestern and southwestern sectors where the runners can be seen cut into the curved tufa wall dividing corridors B and C. These are matched by the grooves along the edges of the rectangular tufa piers. Rectangular travertine blocks fitted with bronze ratchets for operating capstans, originally eight in each sector, are set into the floor of the corridor opposite alternate spaces between the tufa pillars. These blocks usually have a round hole in the centre and often show traces of the bronze socket that

The inner wall of corridor B in the basement. The lift runners passed through the slots in the wall above the arch. The travertine block set into the floor would have had an inset with a round hole in it to house the capstan. The hollowed-out area opposite this block provided room for the handles and capstan.

was fitted into the hole. An almost complete example has survived in one of the flanking tunnels at the southeastern end and can be reconstructed with reasonable certainty. There is a shallow cavity in the curved wall opposite each of the blocks to allow the handles of the capstan to turn. Similar shallow cavities higher up the wall prove that the capstans operated at more than one level in a similar way to those in Nelson's flagship, the *Victory*. A series of joist holes at two levels shows that there were two intermediate floors, one at 1.75 metres and another at 3.5 metres above the basement floor. These intermediate floors did not cross the lift shafts. The placing of the capstan blocks shows a system of alternate capstans and lift shafts.

It can be assumed that these new lifts must have been an afterthought because the new lift shafts did not coincide with the arches in the tufa wall but cut across them in a totally haphazard manner, rendering some of them unusable. The lifts themselves rise to the third level to the point just below the arena where

The tufa wall along the inner side of corridor B in the southwest sector showing the grooves (A) that held the wooden runners for the early lift system. Slots for the cross beams holding the top of the capstan pole in position are shown at B. The brick-work is all of a later date. The concavities in the wall (where the section is taken) that make room for the capstan arms are visible. The groove for a ramp is visible above the arch.

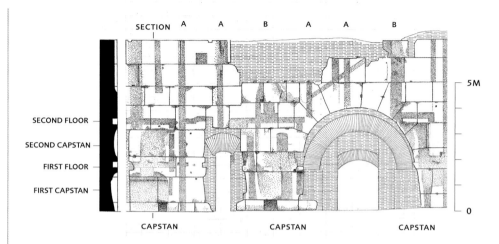

the animals would have been driven up a ramp through a trapdoor into the arena, goaded by the animal handlers standing on a narrow wooden walkway. None of this woodwork survives, but cuttings in the stone tell the whole story. The lifts operating in this corridor could be no more than 1.8 metres square with an internal measurement of somewhat less than this. One could conceivably have got lions and tigers into them but certainly nothing larger.

There is a group of well-preserved tufa piers in the northeastern sector where one can see the grooves for the ramps cut into the lintels above alternate piers. The most practical interpretation is that the lift box rose up as far as the joists supporting the arena floor and that the animal was driven out onto the ramp and up into the arena. The angle of the ramp and the position of the lift would allow a height clearance of about 85 centimetres if the trapdoor in the arena floor was raised to let the animal through but at least 10 centimetres less if the trapdoor was lowered. However, the evidence is

The line of tufa piers along the outer side of corridor B in the northeast sector showing the alternate system of capstans and lifts. Grooves for the upright wooden lift runners (A) can be seen on the edges of the piers. Slots for the cross beams holding the top of the capstan pole in position are shown at B. Vestiges of the ramps sloping up to the arena can be seen along the lintel. The concrete and brick-work is of a later date.

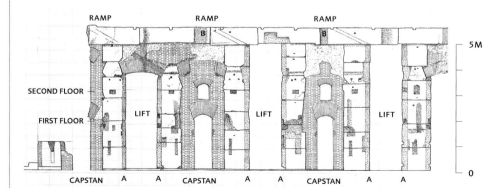

ambiguous as below some of the lintels, where later brick reinforcement survives, one can see clearly that, at least from the time the reinforcing brickwork was inserted, the ramps extended across the lift shafts. Similar traces can be seen on the curved wall. This suggests an alternative but more complicated solution. In this case, the ramp extended right back to the second floor level, obstructing the lift shaft and only allowing it to rise to that level, from which the animal would be driven up the much longer ramp to the arena. The only advantage of this would be a larger trapdoor giving a greater height clearance. The lesser height clearance was probably adequate for most animals but may not have been sufficient for larger ones, such as bears. It may have been possible to modify the system when it was planned to use bigger animals.

Although the new lift system seems to be well designed, it was clearly another change of plan as the arches and doors in the wall dividing corridors B and C do not seem to relate in any rational way to the lift shafts, which often partially or totally block them. The route of the animals to the lifts cannot possibly be along corridor B, which was blocked by the capstans and lifts. It had to be along the 0.5-metre wide corridor A or the 2-metre wide corridor C. However, where the lift shafts did not correspond with an opening in the curved wall it would have had to have been along the narrow corridor A. The D-shaped area D/E with huge arches giving access to C seems a likely holding area for animals.

A model of the lift system in corridor C, seen from behind the tufa piers. The lift box is shown open and ready for loading at ground level (*top*) and raised to the second level above ground (*above*).

The underground animal cages or holding pens were almost certainly made of wood and no trace of them has ever been found, but in the D-shaped area there are the remains of several post sockets. These run parallel to the straight wall and suggest that the area was divided into two, first by a fence and later with a brick wall, which may have been put there to separate the animals from the people operating the scenery and props.

Animals that were too large for the lifts in corridor B would have been taken up to the arena in one of four larger lifts that were installed in the

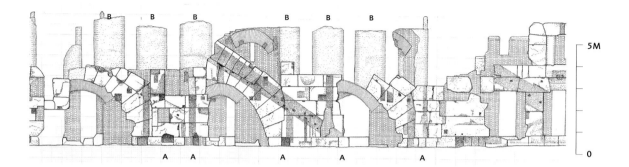

5M

0

Above and right
Part of the south wall of the central corridor in the basement. The stonework dates from the reign of Domitian. The concrete and brickwork are of a later date. This is the best-preserved section, showing an almost complete tufa half-arch. Nowhere has the upper part of these structures survived. The indentation and the holes for attaching the sloping wooden 'shelf' are visible just above the half arch. Perpendicular grooves (A) held the runners for some sort of lift system. The tower-like features in the background (B) are concrete shafts of the later lift system.

corners of the two elongated D-shaped areas at the junction of the curved and straight walls. The curved walls have a most peculiar structure at these points and there are capstan blocks set into the floor there. The tufa wall in the outermost of the straight corridors in the southwestern sector survives right up to the arena level and one can see traces of the enormous ramps at an angle of 30 degrees that led up to the arena. Measuring 3 metres wide, this corridor was definitely large enough to allow animals as big as rhinos and elephants to pass through.

EXPANDING SCENERY
The four walls forming the central main axis corridor H and the corridors on either side, G, make up a single unit, the scenery unfolding down the centre and the capstans for raising it operating in the flanking corridors.

The remains of the complex tufa walls that flanked the central aisle are still clearly visible, although nowhere does the upper part survive. The north side of the corridor is a mirror image of the south side, which is described here. Starting from the west end, corridors A and B were spanned by a tufa arch. Next to this was the entrance to corridor C, now partially blocked by two travertine blocks. There were then two wide rectangular doorways with 'windows' of the same width above them. Beyond this is a 4.5-metre stretch of wall possibly with a 'window' at the upper level. This is followed by a succession of half arches supporting ramps sloping at 30 degrees to the horizontal. The arches rest against upright tufa piers 3.5 metres wide to which they are scarcely bonded, again suggesting an afterthought. There were eight or possibly nine of these features along the whole length of the main axis; it is impossible to be certain as the eastern end is so badly damaged. The system was probably completed with another arch spanning corridors A/B at the eastern end. Clearly the sloping arches supported some scenic system that folded down beneath the arena, but a close examination of the 3.5 metre wide upright tufa pillars shows that a lift system also operated in the central corridor. As it would be impossible for more than one system to operate at the same time one must assume that it was an alternative system. This infinite variety is found all over the basement; one can see where lifts have been moved and ramps extended. This is both typical of and unique to the Colosseum.

The walls forming corridors G on either side of the central corridor are much more difficult to study. These two corridors were later converted to house concrete lift shafts and the lower half of the walls forming corridor F were encased in brick-faced concrete. However, by examining the spaces between the lift shafts and the upper part of the walls facing onto corridor F we can reconstruct both walls with varying degrees of accuracy. They appear to be similar to the walls flanking the west end of the main

The wall along the north side of the central corridor of the basement, showing the remains of one of the tufa half arches of the Domitianic period reinforced with brick.

central corridor H, having wide doorways 2.5 metres high and 1.5–2.0 metres wide, separated by walls of a similar width. They were matched by window-like openings of the same width and 1.5 metres high at the upper level.

The series of half arches, like flying buttresses, with the top sloping upwards at an angle of 30 degrees in the central corridor (H) and the capstans in the corridors on either side of it (G), are all that remains of the mechanism for operating the *pegmata*, the system which raised scenery and props up into the arena and brought them down again as and when required. All the experts agree that there could have been large trapdoors along the central corridor which could be lowered to an angle of 30 degrees. The minimalists argue that trapdoors were lowered, scenery was loaded onto them and they were hoisted up again, but this could hardly produce the spectacular effects described in the ancient sources. The maximalists, myself among them, argue for a much more complex system of expanding scenery.

Seneca, Josephus and a few other Roman authors give us a glimmer of an idea of the fantastic scenic effects that this system of expanding scenery could conjure up 'at the press of a button', but we know very little about how these illusions were created. There is a passage in Apuleius's book *The Golden Ass* where Lucius, the man who has been turned into an ass, enters the theatre at Corinth and describes the opening scene of the games:

> First there was a hill of wood ... reared up exceeding high and garnished
> about with all sort of green verdures and lively trees, from the top
> whereof ran down a clear and fresh fountain, made by the skilled hands
> of the artificer, distilling out waters below. There were a few young and
> tender goats plucking and feeding daintily on the budding grass.

At the end of the scene the arena is cleared and 'by certain engines the ground opened and swallowed up the hill of wood'.

Appuleius's novel is picaresque and allegorical and we have to accept his account as fanciful – no amphitheatre has ever been found at Corinth, for example, even though it was a Roman colony – but it is tempting to think that he drew his description of the scene from personal experience.

There is a minimalist and a maximalist interpretation of the scenic effects the Colosseum was capable of producing from beneath the arena. Some people have argued that it could have come up with not just one hill with a couple of goats on it but a whole range of hills measuring as much as 30×8 metres. There is also the question of height. The trapdoor system proposed by most experts could only produce a height of about three metres.

I have done some experiments with articulated timber structures projecting upwards. This involved long pivoted timbers, sinew or horsehair springs, similar to those used in ancient catapults, capstans and counterweights. The whole system operated like a jack-in-a-box, rising automatically when released but having to be wound back down. The system requires three timber frames. The first, some 9.5 metres long, would be pivoted at the top of the wall. The second frame would rest on the sloping wall. The third piece would rest on a wooden shelf fastened to the wall within the central corridor. Grooves for fitting these shelves and holes for the pins holding them in place can be clearly seen on the inside face of the

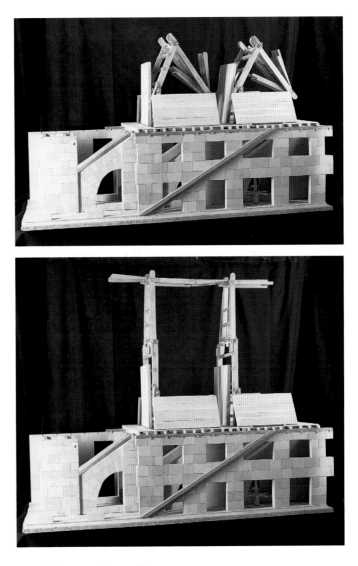

A model of part of the central corridor H and its two flanking corridors G showing the maximalist possibilities for expanding scenery. The framework is shown unfolding (*top*) and erected to its maximum potential (*above*) with a gangway along the top.

wall. A slight change in angle at the junction of the upright wall seems to confirm a hinging at this point. A further piece could either fold back on this or lie on the ground. The model shows the theory in practice with a walkway some 12.5 metres above the arena. It is shown (above) at its maximum potential but it could be adapted to produce a lower elevation. Huge trapdoors would open up above the central corridor and the corridors on either side, allowing the structure to rise from beneath the arena, unfolding as it went. Once raised, the trapdoors would lock the structure into position. Painted scenery, attached to the top of the structure, would unfold as it ascended, covering not only the structure but also the upright trapdoors.

Using this method, it is possible to produce scenery towering as much as 15 metres above the arena. This is the maximum potential of the system. Normally an elevation of 6–10 metres would be more than adequate. To lower the contraption, the painted scenery would be pulled up over the trapdoors from the inside. The trapdoors were then opened wide and the structure wound down beneath the arena. Similar machines mounted on wheels could have been used in the period before the permanent arena was installed.

Being made of wood, no remains of the Colosseum's trapdoors, large or small, have survived. However, the amphitheatre at Capua in southern Italy has yielded some useful data. The substructures beneath the arena here have a system of parallel corridors almost identical to the Colosseum. It was modified much less and the concrete floor of the arena is substantially intact, though the section above the central aisle is missing, and if there were flap-down ramps here there is no longer any trace of them in the masonry. But we do know that there were 62 trapdoors set into the vaulted concrete floor of the arena, and above the two corridors flanking the main aisle there were trapdoors for thirty lifts. There are others, some of them double the normal size, at various points in the arena. As the Colosseum is slightly larger, it may have had more than this.

Traces of the wooden flooring of the Colosseum can be seen where the top of the tufa wall survives in several places. These consist of slots approximately 10 centimetres or 14 centimetres wide and about 1.0–1.5 metres apart. The slots themselves are dovetailed. Beste suggests that these were used to lock wooden beams to the top of the wall and that joists and floor boarding rested on top of these. The great advantage of a wooden floor was that it could be altered easily, enabling the producers of a show to create unexpected special effects.

APPENDIX II
WRITING ABOUT
THE COLOSSEUM

Many writers, poets, historians and even scientists have been moved to record their impressions of the Colosseum over the years. Presented here are some extracts from Gibbon, Byron, Shelley, Goethe, Dickens and the botonist, Richard Deakin, all of whom were writing in the eighteenth and nineteenth centuries, before the Amphitheare was the cleaned and restored structure visitors encounter today.

In the mid-eighteenth century the twin cities of Pompeii and Herculenium were discovered almost intact under a blanket of volcanic ash in the Bay of Naples. They had been buried following the eruption of Mount Vesuvius in AD 79, one year before the inauguration of the Colosseum, and their discovery helped to spark a new popular enthusiasm in the classical world. Many people embarked on what came to be known as the 'Grand Tour' of ancient sites, and the English historian Edward Gibbon (1737-94), who visited Rome for the first time at the age of 25, was among them. He wrote graphically of the Colosseum's bloody spectacles in his classic history, *The Decline and Fall of the Roman Empire* (1776-88). In the following extract Gibbon describes the antics of the emperor Commodus, who fancied himself as a beast hunter and gladiator in the Amphitheatre.

Every sentiment of virtue and humanity was extinct in the mind of Commodus. Whilst he thus abandoned the reins of empire to these unworthy favourites, he valued nothing in sovereign power, except the unbounded licence of indulging his sensual appetites. His hours were spent in a seraglio of three hundred beautiful women, and as many boys, of every rank, and of every province; and, wherever the arts of seduction proved ineffectual, the brutal lover had recourse to violence. The ancient historians have expatiated on these abandoned scenes of prostitution, which scorned every restraint of nature or modesty; but it would not be easy to translate their too faithful descriptions into the decency of modern language. The intervals of lust were filled up with the basest amusements....

... Commodus, from his earliest infancy, discovered an aversion to whatever was rational or liberal, and a fond attachment to the amusements of the populace; the sports of the circus and amphitheatre, the combats of gladiators, and the hunting of wild beasts....

... On the appointed day, the various motives of flattery, fear, and curiosity, attracted to the amphitheatre an innumerable multitude of spectators; and some degree of applause was deservedly bestowed on the uncommon skill of the Imperial performer. Whether he aimed at the head or heart of the animal, the wound was alike certain and mortal. With arrows, whose point was shaped into the form of a crescent, Commodus often intercepted the rapid career, and cut asunder the long bony neck of the ostrich. A panther was let loose; and the archer waited until he had leaped upon a trembling malefactor. In the same instant the shaft flew, the beast dropt dead, and the man remained unhurt. The dens of the amphitheatre disgorged at once a hundred lions; a hundred darts from the unerring hand of Commodus laid them dead as they ran raging round the *Arena*. Neither the huge bulk of the elephant, nor the scaly hide of the rhinoceros, could defend them from his stroke....

But the meanest of the populace were affected with shame and indignation when they beheld their sovereign enter the lists as a gladiator, and glory in a profession which the laws and manners of the Romans had branded with the justest note of infamy. He chose the habit and arms of the *Secutor*, whose combat with the *Retiarius* formed one of the most lively scenes in the bloody sports of the amphitheatre. The *Secutor* was armed with an helmet, sword, and buckler; his naked antagonist had only a large net and a trident; with the one he endeavoured the entangle, with the other to dispatch, his enemy. If he missed the first throw, he was obliged to fly from the pursuit of the *Secutor*, till he had prepared his net for a second cast. The emperor fought in this character seven hundred and thirty-five several times. These glorious achievements were carefully recorded in the public acts of the empire; and that he might omit no circumstance of infamy, he received from the common fund of gladiators, a stipend so exorbitant, that it became a new and most ignominious tax upon the Roman people.

The German poet, dramatist and scholar Johann Wolfgang von Goethe (1749-1832) spent two years in Italy. He described one of his visits to the Colosseum in his *Travels in Italy, France and Switzerland* published in 1787.

Of the beauty of a walk through Rome by moonlight it is impossible to form a conception, without having witnessed it. All single objects are swallowed up by the great masses of light and shade, and nothing but grand and general outlines present themselves to the eye. For three several days we have enjoyed to the full the brightest and most glorious nights. Peculiarly beautiful, at such a time, is the Coliseum. At night it is always closed. A hermit dwells in a little shrine within its range, and beggars of all kinds nestle beneath its crumbling arches: the latter had lit a fire on the arena, and a gentle wind bore down the smoke to the ground, so that the lower portion of the ruins was quite hid by it; while, above, the vast walls stood out in deeper darkness before the eye. As we stopped at the gate to contemplate the scene through the iron gratings, the moon shone brightly in the heavens above. Presently the smoke found its way up the sides, and through every chink and opening, while the moon lit it up like a cloud. The sight was exceedingly glorious.

The German polymath Johann Wolfgang von Goethe visited the Colosseum several times in the late 1780s.

The English poet Lord Byron (1788-1824), who settled in Italy towards the end of his life, described the Amphitheatre's ruined arena after dark in his verse-drama *Manfred* (1817), which was inspired by the Colosseum.

> When I was wandering,—upon such a night
> I stood within the Coliseum's wall,
> Midst the chief relics of almighty Rome;
> The trees which grew along the broken arches
> Waved dark in the blue midnight, and the stars
> Shone through the rents of ruin; from afar
> The watchdog bay'd beyond the Tiber; and
> More near from out the Caesars' palace came
> The owl's long cry, and, interruptedly,
> Of distant sentinels the fitful song
> Begun and died upon the gentle wind.
> Some cypresses beyond the time-worn breach

Appear'd to skirt the horizon, yet they stood
Within a bowshot—Where the Caesars dwelt,
And dwell the tuneless birds of night, amidst
A grove which springs through levell's battlements,
And twines its roots with the imperial hearths,
Ivy usurps the laurel's place of growth; —
But the gladiators' bloody Circus stands,
A noble wreck in ruinous perfection!
While Caesar's chambers, and the Augustan halls,
Grovel on earth in indistinct decay. —
And thou didst shine, thou rolling moon, upon
All this, and cast a wide and tender light,
Which soften'd down the hoar austerity
Of rugged desolation, and fill'd up,
As 'twere anew, the gaps of centuries;
Leaving that beautiful which still was so,
And making that which was not, till the place
Became religion, and the heart ran o'er
With silent worship of the great of old! —
The dead, but sceptred sovereigns, who still rule
Our spirits from their urns. —

Byron's epic poem *Childe Harold's Pilgrimage* (1812-18) also contains a long description of the Colosseum, which closes with the following passage.

But here, where Murder breathed her bloody steam: —
And here, where buzzing nations choked the ways,
And roared or murmured like a mountain stream
Dashing or winding as its torrent strays;
Here, where the Roman million's blame or praise
Was Death or Life — the plaything of a crowd —
My voice sounds much — and fall the stars' faint rays
On the arena void — seats crushed — walls bowed —
And galleries, where my steps seem echoes strangely loud....
But when the rising moon begins to climb
Its topmost arch, and gently pauses there —
When the stars twinkle through the loops of Time,
And the low night-breeze waves along the air

The garland-forest, which the grey walls wear,
Like laurels on the bald first Caesar's head —
When the light shines serene but doth not glare —
Then in this magic circle raise the dead;
Heroes have trod this spot — 'tis on their dust
    ye tread.

Byron's great friend, the English poet Percy Bysshe Shelley (1792-1822), lived in Italy from 1818, and in that year set out his own impressions of the Flavian Amphitheatre in a letter to Thomas Love Peacock.

Lord Byron described the Colosseum in *Manfred* and *Childe Harold's Pilgrimage*.

The Coliseum is unlike any work of human hands I ever saw before. It is of enormous height and circuit, and the arches built of massive stones are piled on one another, and jut into the blue air, shattered into the forms of overhanging rocks. It has been changed by time into an amphitheatre of rocky hills overgrown by the wild olive, the myrtle, and the fig tree, and threaded by little paths, which wind among its ruined stairs and immeasurable galleries: the copsewood overshadows you as you wander through its labyrinths, and the wild weeds of this climate of flowers bloom under your feet. The arena is covered with grass, and pierces, like the skirts of a natural plain, the chasms of the broken arches around. But a small part of the exterior circumferance remains – it is exquisitely light and beautiful... the interior is all ruin. I can scarcely believe that when encrusted with Dorian marble and ornamented by columns of Egyptian granite, its effect could have been so sublime and so impressive... it is open to the sky, and it was the clear and sunny weather of the end of November... when we visited it, day after day.

The English novelist Charles Dickens (1812-70) visited Rome in 1844 and published his thoughts about the Colosseum in his *Pictures from Italy* two years later.

It is no fiction, but plain, sober, honest Truth, to say: so suggestive and distinct is it [the Colosseum] at this hour: that, for a moment – actually in passing in – they who will, may have the whole great pile before them,

Charles Dickens visited the Colosseum in 1844.

as it used to be, with thousands of eager faces staring down into the arena, and such a whirl of strife, and blood, and dust, going on down there, as no language can describe. Its solitude, its awful beauty, and its utter desolation, strike upon the stranger, the next moment, like a softened sorrow; and never in his life, perhaps, will he be so moved and overcome by any sight, not immediately connected with his own affections and afflictions.

To see it crumbling there, an inch a year; its walls and arches overgrown with green; its corridors open to the day; the long grass growing in its porches; young trees of yesterday, springing up on its ragged parapets, and bearing fruit: chance produce of the seeds dropped there by the birds who build their nests within its chinks and crannies; to see its Pit of Fight filled up with earth, and the peaceful Cross planted in the centre; to climb into its upper halls, and look down on ruin, ruin, ruin, all about it... It is the most impressive, the most stately, the most solemn, grand, majestic, mournful sight, conceivable. Never, in its bloodiest prime, can the sight of the gigantic Coliseum, full and running over with the lustiest life, have moved one heart, as it must move all who look upon it now, a ruin. GOD be thanked: a ruin!

...Beneath the church of St. Giovanni and St. Paolo, there are the jaws of a terrific range of caverns, hewn out of the rock, and said to have another outlet underneath the Coliseum – tremendous darknesses of vast extent, half-buried in the earth and unexplorable, where the dull torches, flashed by the attendants, glimmer down long ranges of distant vaults branching to the right and left, like streets in a city of the dead; and show the cold damp stealing down the walls, drip-drop, drip-drop, to join the pools of water that lie here and there, and never saw, and never will see, one ray of the sun. Some accounts make these the prisons of the wild beasts destined for the amphitheatre; some, the prisons of the condemned gladiators; some, both. But the legend most appalling to the fancy is, that in the upper range (for there are two stories of these caves) the Early Christians destined to be eaten at the Coliseum Shows, heard the wild beasts, hungry for them, roaring down below; until, upon the night and solitude of their captivity, there burst the sudden noon and life of the vast theatre crowded to the parapet, and of these, their dreaded neighbours, bounding in!

In 1871 the Italian archaeologist Pietro Rosa was given permission to clear the Colosseum of the vegetation that clung to its ruins. Less than two decades earlier, the English botanist Richard Deakin published his *Flora of the Colosseum* (1855), which catalogued for posterity the enormous variety of trees and plants that had made the building their home for more than a thousand years.

Richard Deakin's own illustration of a caper tree sprouting out of a ruined column from his *Flora of the Colosseum* (1855).

> The plants which we have found growing upon the Coloseum... amount to no less a number than 420 species; in this number there are examples of 253 Genera, and illustrations of 66 of the Natural Orders of plants, a number which seems almost incredible. There are 56 species of Grasses – 47 of the order *Compositoe* or Syngenesious plants – and 41 of the Leguminous or Pea tribe: but it must be remembered that, though the ground occupied by the building is about six acres, the surface of the walls and lodgement on the ruins upon which they grow is much more extensive, and the variety of soil is much greater, than would be supposed without examination; for, on the lower north side, it is damp, and favourable to the production of many plants, while the upper walls and accumulated mould are warmer and dryer, and, consequently, better suited for the development of others: and, on the south side, it is hot and dry, and suited only for the growth of differently constructed tribes.
>
> The collection of the plants and species noted has been made some years; but since that time, many of the plants have been destroyed, from the alterations and restorations that have been made in the ruins; a circumstance that cannot but be lamented. To preserve a further falling of any portion is most desirable; but to carry the restorations, and the brushing and cleaning, to the extent to which it has been subjected, instead of leaving it in its wild and solemn grandeur, is to destroy the impression and solitary lesson which so magnificent a ruin is calculated to make upon the mind....

GLOSSARY

amphitheatre Literally, a double theatre with seating totally surrounding the performance area.

Amphitheatrum Flavium The amphitheatre built by the Flavian emperors, Vespasian, Titus and Domitian. The Romans knew it simply as the Amphitheatre. Later it became known as the Colosseum.

andabatae Heavily armoured cavalry who wore visored helmets without eyeholes and charged blindly at each other.

Appian Way The first of Rome's great trunk roads built by Appius Claudius in 312 BC. The road stretched from Rome to Capua, a distance of 184 kilometres.

armamentarium The weapons store for the Colosseum close to the Ludus Magnus and the Ludus Dacicus.

bestiarii People who fought wild beasts in the arena.

bipedales Thin bricks two Roman feet (60 centimetres) square.

cavea Seating area of a theatre or amphitheatre.

circus Stadium for chariot racing. The Circus Maximus was the oldest entertainment venue in Rome and was often used for animal hunts.

consuls The two chief Roman magistrates. They held their office for one year only and were originally elected by the people but during the empire they could only hold office with the emperor's approval.

cornua Large metal horns played by army musicians and in the amphitheatre.

crupellarius A very heavily armed Gallic gladiator.

cunei Literally, 'wedges'; seating areas in the amphitheatre.

deus ex machina Mechanical system for lowering gods onto the stage and removing the again used in Greek theatres. It involved the use of cranes.

Domus Aurea Literally, 'Golden House'. The great palace built by Nero after the fire of AD 64. The remains of part of it can still be seen today on the hill side just north of the Colosseum.

editor One who puts on public entertainment.

essedaria Female gladiator who fought from a chariot. This type of gladiator came from Britain.

familia gladiatoria Group of gladiators under the control of one man.

First Triumvirate Name given to the political alliance formed in 60 BC by Rome's three most powerful men, Julius Caesar, Pompey the Great and the wealthy businessman Marcus Licinius Crassus, to control the government of Rome.

Forma Urbis Romae The great marble plan of Rome showing the ground plan of every building, set up in the Forum of Peace at the end of the second century AD.

Forum The market and place for political assembly in the centre of Rome between the Palatine Hill and the Capitol where the politicians addressed the people and the tribes voted. It was also the centre of commerce, and law courts were here too.

galerus   Large shoulder guard worn by a *retiarius*.

Gaul   Main area occupied by the Celtic tribes including northern Italy and the whole of modern France. It was also the name given to a member of one of these tribes and (originally) gladiators drawn from their number.

gladius   Sword used by the Roman legions which was also used by most gladiators.

greave   Metal leg guard.

hoplomachus   Gladiator, probably of Greek origin, armed with a helmet, a right arm-guard, long greaves, a small round shield and a sword.

lanista   Trainer of gladiators.

laquerarius   Obscure type of gladiator who probably fought with a lasso.

lictor   Attendant who accompanied a Roman magistrate carrying a bundle of rods and an axe symbolising the magistrate's power to inflict corporal and capital punishment.

ludus   Training school for gladiators or beast fighters. The most famous were the Ludus Magnus, Ludus Dacicus and the Ludus Matutinus, all located at the east end of the Colosseum. The last of these was the training school for the beast fighters.

maenianum   Seating level, equivalent to the stalls or circle, in an amphitheatre. There were four such levels in the Colosseum known, in order of decreasing importance, as *maenianum primum, maenianum secundum immum, maenianum secundum summum* and *maenianum secundum in ligneis*. The last of these was right at the top.

manica   Segmented metal armguard.

munus, pl. *munera*   Gladiatorial show or shows.

murmillo   Kind of fish. The name was applied to a type of gladiator who had an image of a fish on his helmet.

naumachia   Mock naval battle. The name was also applied to the place where such events took place.

nymphaeum   Ornamental fountain.

opus signinum   Type of waterproof cement used for lining aqueducts, cisterns and swimming pools.

paegnarii   Mock and often comic gladiators used to warm up the crowd before the real fights took place.

parma, parmula   Small round shield.

parma equestris   Originally, the round shield used by the Roman cavalry from the fourth to the second century BC. It was later used by mounted gladiators.

parmularii   Gladiators, such as Thracians, armed with small shields as distinguished from *scutarii* who were armed with large shields. Caligula and Titus were both avid supporters of the *parmularii*.

patricians   The original ruling class of Rome.

pegmata   The scenic system that rose up from beneath the floor of the arena.

plebeians, plebs   The original lower class of Rome. By as early as the fifth century BC wealthy *plebeians* were being elected consuls and in 367 BC a law was passed which ensured that at least one of the two consuls each year must be a *plebeian*. This made the distinction between *plebeian* and *patrician* meaningless, although modern historians continue to refer to the Roman lower classes a *plebs*.

pollice verso   Literally 'turned thumb'. The signal for death in the arena. In the popular imagination this is assumed to mean 'thumbs down' but this is highly unlikely. It may mean 'thumb forward', as if stabbing someone.

pompa   Ceremonial procession.

praetor   Roman magistrate ranked just below consul.

provocator   Gladiator type derived from the Roman legionary. He was armed with a helmet, shield and sword based on the current legionary type.

retiarius   Lightly armed gladiator who fought with a net and trident.

rudis   Wooden practice sword used by gladiators. It was also the name of the wooden sword given to a gladiator on retirement after a distinguished career in the arena.

sagitarius   An archer.

Samnite   An early type of gladiator originating in Campania in the southern Italy.

Saturnalia   The festival of Saturn held over several days in mid-winter beginning on 17 December. Gladiatorial games were held as part of this festival.

scutarii   Gladiators such as *murmillones* armed with large shields as distinguished from *parmularii* armed with small shields. Nero and Domitian were both avid fans of the *scutarii*.

scutum   Large shield originating in Italy and used by legionaries and some gladiators.

secutor   Literally 'pursuer'. The gladiator armed with egg-shaped helmet, large shield and sword who normally fought the *retiarius*.

Senate   The permanent political assembly at Rome, an advisory body composed of ex-magistrates.

servus   A slave.

sica   The curved dagger used by Thracian gladiators.

spectacula   Performances, particularly by gladiators.

spoliarium   The place where dead gladiators were stripped of their armour.

stagnum   A pool or lake.

tessera   A token or ticket giving access to the Amphitheatre.

Thracian   A very popular type of gladiator originating in Thrace (modern Bulgaria). He was armed with a small shield and a curved dagger (*sica*).

travertine   A hard white limestone used in many buildings at Rome, particularly the Colosseum.

tribunes   Plebeian magistrates elected by the plebeians to protect their rights. They had the power to veto laws.

tufa   A soft brownish volcanic stone.

velarium   The awning used in theatres and amphitheatres to protect the spectators from the sun. The *velarium* at the Colosseum was hoisted up by local sailors.

velites   Roman light armed troops armed with javelins. Also the name of similarly armed gladiators.

venationes   Wild animal hunts.

venatores   Wild animal hunters.

veteranus   Literally a 'veteran' – an experienced gladiator.

FURTHER READING

The poet Martial is the only ancient author who provides an eyewitness account of the building and opening of the Colosseum. His *Liber de Spectaculis*, a short book of epigrams written to celebrate the opening of the building in AD 80, is couched in a flowery poetic style that is often difficult to understand, but is nevertheless a fund of information. Relying on imperial patronage, Martial praises the emperor's works regardless of how bad they are. His fawning attitude to Vespasian's son Domitian resulted in his permanent fall from grace when that emperor was assassinated and condemned. *Liber de Spectaculis* is available in a dual text edition (Latin and English) in the Loeb Classical Library, Martial Vol. 1 (Harvard University Press, 1993).

The vast majority of modern literature on the Colosseum is in Italian. *The Colosseum*, originally published in Italian by Electa in 2000 and by the J. Paul Getty Museum in English translation in 2001, is an authoritative collection of academic articles on various aspects of the Colosseum edited by Ada Gabucci and is essential reading for anyone interested in the subject.

David L. Bomgardner's *The History of the Roman Amphitheatre* (Routledge, 2000) is an excellent guide to amphitheatres in general and covers all amphitheatres with substantial remains. Bomgardner gives details such as seating capacity, arena size and other facilities, and thereby enables comparisons to be made between various amphitheathres in different parts of the Roman world.

There is no shortage of good books in English on gladiators and the games. Roland Auguet's excellent *Cruelty and Civilization: The Roman Games* (Routledge, 1994) originally appeared in French more than 30 years ago and surveys the whole subject – gladiators, beast hunts and chariot racing – and examines the effects of these on Roman society. Keith Hopkins's *Death and Renewal* (Cambridge, 1983) has a short but valuable section on gladiators. The late Thomas Wiedemann's excellent *Emperors and Gladiators* (Routledge, 1992) and Donald G. Kyle's *Spectacles of Death in Ancient Rome* (Routledge, 1998) both look at various aspects of the games. Carlin A. Barton's *The Sorrows of the Ancient Romans: The Gladiator and the Monster* (Princeton University Press, 1993) is also recommended. The catalogue to the British Museum's exhibition *Gladiators and Caesars* by E. Kohne and C. Ewigleben (British Museum Press, 2000) is a very important contribution to the literature as it includes a wealth of colour illustrations of gladiatorial equipment and ancient representations of gladiators. It also includes several of Junkelmann's reconstructions. An enormous number of articles on various aspects of the Colosseum and the games have been published in academic journals. Many of these can be traced through the bibliographies of Bomgardner, Kyle and Wiedemann.

For those with a more general interest in the ancient city of Rome, several books can be recommended. *The Oxford Archaeological Guide to Rome* (Oxford, 1998) by Amanda Claridge, a former assistant director at the British School at Rome and an expert on Roman history, is by far the best archaeological guide. Although aimed at serious scholars, it is a mine of information for the general reader. *The Ancient City: Life in Classical Athens and Rome* (Oxford, 1998) by Peter Connolly and Hazel Dodge illustrates the development of Rome with the help of reconstructions of dozens of buildings. It shows the Roman Forum at various stages of its development and traces the evolution of the theatre from Athens to Rome.

William J. MacDonald's *The Architecture of the Roman Empire: An Introductory Study* (Yale, 1965), although a little out of date, is still a very good book for students and includes chapters on the palaces of Nero and Domitian. *Ancient Rome: The Archaeology of the Eternal City* (Oxford, 2000) by Hazel Dodge and John Coulston is another very informative academic title. (Dodge is an authority on Roman building materials, particularly marble.)

Roman Military Equipment (Shire Publications, 1993) by Mike Bishop and Jon Coulston is by far the best book on Roman armour and weaponry. Bishop is totally committed to the subject and is the editor of the *Journal of Roman Military Equipment Studies*. Finally, Peter Connolly's *Greece and Rome at War* (Greenhill Books, 1998, revised edition) is useful as a general guide to the development of armour, weaponry, military organization and tactics in the Greaco-Roman world.

*　　　*　　　*

A Note on the Quotations

Most of the extracts from classical works used to illustrate the present text are quoted from the Loeb Classical Library editions (Harvard University Press): p.9 St Augustine of Hippo, *Confessions* (trans. W. Watts, 1631; rev. 1912); pp.20 and 148 Suetonius, *The Lives of the Caesars* (trans. J. C. Rolfe, 1913); pp.23 and 120 Tacitus, *Annals* (trans. J. Jackson, 1937); pp.32, 136 and 146 Martial, *Liber de Spectaculis* (trans. D. R. Shackleton Bailey, 1993); p.71 Livy, *The History of Rome* (trans. B. O. Foster, 1919); pp.79 and 81–2 Juvenal, *The Satires* (trans. G. G. Ramsay, 1918); p.107 Lucilius, *Fragments* (trans. E. H. Warmington, 1938); p.121 Strabo, *Geography* (trans. H. L. Jones, 1932); p.123 Tacitus, *Histories* (trans. C. H. Moore, 1925); pp.123 and 124 Pliny the Younger, *Letters* X, 96 and 97 (trans. B. Radice, 1969); pp.134, 148 and 154 Cassius Dio, *Roman History* (E. Cary, 1914); p.204 Apuleius, *The Golden Ass* (trans. W. Adlington, 1566; rev. S. Gaselee, 1915). Extracts from Tertullian's *On Spectacles* on pp.68–9, 118 and 133 are from the T. & T. Clarke edition (1899). W. H. Auden's translation of Goethe's *Travels in Italy* (quoted on p.209) is published by HarperCollins Publishers (1962).

INDEX

PICTURE CREDITS

BBC Worldwide would like to thank the following individuals and organizations for providing photographs and for permission to reproduce copyright material. While every effort has been made to trace and acknowledge copyright holders, we would like to apologize should there be any errors or omissions.

Key: *l* left; *r* right; *t* top; *b* bottom. Page 1 Bibliothèque Nationale de France; 2–3 Photo Scala, Florence; 5 (*top and third*) Photo Scala, Florence; 6 (*from top to bottom*) Photo Scala, Florence; akg-images, London; Photo Scala, Florence; Electa, Milan 2000/Staatliche Museum, Berlin; 10–11 Photo Scala, Florence; 19 Photo Scala, Florence; 21 Museo Archeologico Nazionale, Naples/Bridgeman Art Library, London; 23 Corbis; 24 akg-images/Erich Lessing; 25 Corbis; 27 akg-images/Erich Lessing; 28 Corbis; 33 Electa, Milan, 2000; 35 Alinari Picture Library; 36 Photo Scala, Florence; 40*r* Electa, Milan, 2000/Giuseppe Schiavinotto, Roma; 46–7 Corbis; 49 Index, Firenze; 57 Corbis; 58*l* Photo Scala, Florence; 60 Photo Scala, Florence; 63 akg-images/Erich Lessing; 66–7 Photo Scala, Florence; 72 Photo Scala, Florence; 73 akg-images, London; 74 British Museum, BR 1919.6-20.4; 77 Roman Museum Augusta Raurica, Augst, Switzerland; 78 Musée d'Arles, photo: Michel Lacanuad; 79 Archivo Fotográfico, Museo Arqueológico Nacional, Madrid; 80 Corbis; 82 British Museum, GR 1117; 85 Musée Romain, photo: J. Zbinden Bern; 86 Photo Scala, Florence; 110–11 Photo Scala, Florence; 113 Musée Archéologique d'Hippone, Algeria; 114 akg-images/Erich Lessing; 115–16 akg-images/Gilles Mermet; 118 Corbis; 121 Corbis; 125 Vatican Library, Rome, Ms Greco, 1613, fol. 258; 129 Corbis; 131 Staatliche Antikensammlungen und Glyptothek, Munich; 135 Werner Forman Archive; 136 Photo Scala, Florence; 138–9 akg-images, London; 141 Roberto Luciani/De Agostini, Milano; 147 Corbis; 152–3 Photo Scala, Florence; 157 Photo Scala, Florence; 162 Courtesy of the University of London, photo: Ian Bavington Jones; 163 Photo Vasari, Rome; 165*b* Photo Vasari, Rome; 167 Hulton Archive; 168 Photo Vasari, Rome; 170–1 Electa, Milan, 2000/Staatliche Museum, Berlin; 173 Electa, Milan, 2000/Museo del Prado, Madrid; 175 Electa, Milan, 2000/Ecole Nationale Superieuere des Beaux Arts, Paris (artist: Carlo Lucangeli); 178 Roberto Luciani/De Agostini, Milano; 181 Electa, Milan, 2000/SAR, Rome; 195 Electa, Milan, 2000; 209 Hermitage, St. Petersburg, Russia/Bridgeman Art Library; 211 Stapleton Collection, UK/ Bridgeman Art Library; 212 Hulton Archive; 213 Richard Deakin, *Flora of the Colosseum*, 1855.

Photographs and artwork on the following pages copyright © Peter Connolly: 5 (*second and fourth*), 15, 22, 30–1, 41, 43, 52, 53, 54–5, 58*r*, 69, 70, 75, 88–9, 90, 91, 93, 94, 96, 97, 98 (*both*), 100, 101, 103, 108, 126–7, 143, 180, 186, 187, 188, 189, 190, 192, 197, 198, 199, 200 (*both*), 201 (*both*), 202 (*both*), 203 and 205 (*both*).

Photographs on the following pages copyright © Christopher Tinker: 17, 40*l*, 44, 48, 51, 59, 61, 62, 64, 65, 104, 150, 155, 159, 165*t* (*both*), 177, 182 and 196.